WILLIAM HENRY HARRISON.

ULYSSES S. GRANT.

RUTHERFORD BIRCHARD HAYES.

JAMES ABRAM GARFIELD.

BENJAMIN HARRISON.

WILLIAM McKINLEY.

THE OHIO PRESIDENTS.

Ohio
and Her Western Reserve
with a Story of Three States

Leading to the Latter, from Connecticut, by
Way of Wyoming, Its Indian Wars and Massacres

by
Alfred Mathews

Member of the Ohio State Archaeological and Historical Society
Member of the Historical Society of Pennsylvania, etc.

WITH ILLUSTRATIONS AND MAPS

HERITAGE BOOKS
2008

HERITAGE BOOKS
AN IMPRINT OF HERITAGE BOOKS, INC.

Books, CDs, and more—Worldwide

For our listing of thousands of titles see our website
at
www.HeritageBooks.com

A Facsimile Reprint
Published 2008 by
HERITAGE BOOKS, INC.
Publishing Division
100 Railroad Ave. #104
Westminster, Maryland 21157

Originally published 1902
New York

— Publisher's Notice —
In reprints such as this, it is often not possible to remove blemishes from the original. We feel the contents of this book warrant its reissue despite these blemishes and hope you will agree and read it with pleasure.

International Standard Book Numbers
Paperbound: 978-0-7884-1869-3
Clothbound: 978-0-7884-7208-4

To the Memory of my Father,

THE LATE

SAMUEL HUNTINGTON MATHEWS, M. D.,

OF PAINESVILLE, OF CLEVELAND, AND OF CALIFORNIA
—ONE OF THE "ARGONAUTS OF '49," WHO ASSISTED
IN EXTENDING TO THE PACIFIC COAST THE PATH
WHICH THE GENERATION OF HIS ANCESTORS HAD
OPENED FROM NEW ENGLAND TO THE SHORES OF LAKE
ERIE—ONE OF THE FIRST-BORN OF THE PIONEERS,
AND, IN CULTURE, CONSCIENCE, COURAGE, IN MANLI-
NESS AND MODESTY, A HIGH TYPE OF THE INCON-
SPICUOUS BUT STERLING CITIZENRY OF THE PURITAN
CONNECTICUT STOCK IN THE WESTERN RESERVE,

THIS LITTLE BOOK
IS AFFECTIONATELY INSCRIBED BY
THE AUTHOR.

PREFACE

THE theme of these pages is twofold: a duality of endeavors, exhibiting a contrast of means, and yet reaching a community of outcome.

Ohio—now arrrived at the centennial of statehood—was resultant from the foregathering of a great number of diverse fragments finally compacted and fused in a homogenous whole by various causes. As the most composite State in the Union, it was formed by the concentrated march of an army of occupation from all of the States. These elements, widely variant as they were, had one principle in common—an inherent conviction of the righteousness of freedom, which led some to dictate, and all to assent to, a basic law against the extension of slavery.

The Western Reserve of Connecticut in

Ohio and Her Western Reserve

Ohio, the largest and most distinctly individualized and most influential of all the varied elements in this composite population, was resultant from the sole energy of the people of a single State. Herein the history of the Reserve forms a contrast with that of Ohio. And both because of its intrinsic interest and the generally inadequate understanding of the power and the peculiarity of Connecticut's wonderful Western expansion, which reached its culmination in the Reserve, the subject is considered here—and, it is believed, for the first time—in all of its connections, from the inception of the ideas of liberty and colonial expansion in old Connecticut, through the strange, wild warfare in Wyoming, Pa., to the realization of the essential ideals of a progressive Puritanism in the "New Connecticut" of Ohio.

Ohio's remarkable rise from the position of a pioneer and backwoods State to one of power and prestige absolutely unequaled, for a long period, by any other in the sisterhood of commonwealths, will be found by final analysis to be predicated, in the main, unmistakably upon Law. By this is of course

Preface

meant fundamental, creating, organizing, and controlling Law as contradistinguished from that irresponsible individualism of action which, however much of enthusiasm and of energy it may employ, however admirable it may be in many of its aims and even outcomes, is nevertheless Anarchy.

Ohio was builded wiser than its builders knew, upon the Ordinance of 1787, that surpassingly wise enactment of early Congress, which was only less important than the Constitution of the United States, and which may not improperly be regarded as the "Ordinance of Freedom" for the whole nation, rather than merely for the old Northwest Territory, if we look upon it as illuminated by the glowing light of 1861–'65, instead of in the pale, but prophetic gleaming of a new dawn in the primitive days of the nation and the Northwest.

If we reflect that the old Northwest Territory was made, morally, what it was by the operation of the great ordinance; that it was primarily a force for the sifting out from the people of the whole country of those opposed to slavery, and their concentration and devel-

Ohio and Her Western Reserve

opment in the Territory; and then recall that Ohio alone, the first State of the Territory when the war came on that resulted in the suppression of slavery, contributed more men to the Union army than Great Britain ever put in the field, even in the greatest and latest of her wars, we begin to apprehend the vast ultimate momentousness of the Ordinance of 1787.

Those who were to become the very first pioneers of Ohio dictated and secured the passage of that ordinance, and its first effect was in making a cosmopolitan commonwealth, rather than a mere extension of a single colony, the population they pioneered into the wilderness. Ohio, owing to the provisions of the ordinance, was the first ground in the United States on which met and eventually merged the people of all the colonies—the first on which the Cavalier and the Puritan and the Quaker stood side by side; the first on which the differentiated strains of blood in the sons of the Carolinas and Virginia, of Maryland and Pennsylvania, of Massachusetts and Connecticut, commingled in a common people.

Preface

And not only did it obtain these many valuable, because varied, elements of population, but, by the operation of the ordinance, *the best of each*—the more morally advanced, as proved by their attitude toward slavery, two generations before it had become a paramount public issue.

It is along the development of these lines, as a study in population and, in the larger sense, of politics, also as an analysis of causes and consequences extending down to the chronicling of a great many definite results, that the history of Ohio here proceeds, rather than as a minute account of those minor incidents, interesting enough in themselves, but which have little of causative significance.

The history of Ohio, as here related, is, therefore, a consideration of many peoples in one State, while the chapters which precede those on Ohio proper, pertaining to the largest, though not the earliest single element that found a home within, and helped to constitute the State, form a study of one people in three States. That portion of the work which treats of the Connecticut westward expansion reveals, therefore, in this respect,

Ohio and Her Western Reserve

as has been said, a contrast with the theme of the other chapters.

But this is by no means the most important contrast which is presented between the subjects of the two sections of the work. The settlement of Ohio proceeded in orderliness and peace and with huge attendant rapidity, success, and prosperity, because it was inaugurated deliberately upon an entirely lawful and planned basis, which prepared the way for stability before the soil was pressed by a pioneer footstep. In the other migratory movement, that tremendously vigorous westward push by Connecticut people which gave the initiative to the whole organized internal colonial movement and which ultimately planted by all odds the largest and strongest and most characteristic single, compact colony in the West (and the "last distinct footprint of Puritanism"), there was at the outset—in the Pennsylvania endeavor—a marked lack of regard for safe legal initiative and procedure, with consequent anarchical conditions and a failure that fell not far short of being complete.

It was a singular mistake for Connecticut

Preface

men to make; altogether contrary to their predominant characteristics of prudence and of practicality. Its occurrence is, in the main, to be attributed to preliminary conditions which almost certainly would have misled any people, and to the non-existence of any precedent whatever for the manner of execution of their really heroic enterprise. But if they partially failed once, in Pennsylvania, because their pathway was not fully paved with law, they splendidly atoned for it with their careful and elaborate preparation for the later movement into that part of the Northwest Territory which was to become Ohio, and the losses of Wyoming were fully compensated in the Western Reserve.

If it may temporarily appear to any reader that the other principal early elements of Ohio's population suffer any injustice in these pages through not being accorded a separate treatment, the cause for dissatisfaction will probably either wholly disappear or greatly diminish, when they find that the story of these elements is more intimately and inseparably interwoven with the founding and the organization of the State, and that they are given

Ohio and Her Western Reserve

ample attention in the chapters devoted to it where the chronicling of their respective shares in the great work becomes not only appropriate but imperative.

It was the people who formed the small though sterling Massachusetts colony who dictated the great ordinance and made the first organized settlement within the limits of the future State. It was the Virginia element, most of whose pioneers came to Chillicothe by way of Kentucky, that was foremost in founding the State under the ægis of the Jeffersonian Democracy, and it was the New Jersey element under General John Cleves Symmes, the founder of Cincinnati, who prominently seconded the successful endeavors of the former. Both of these, and the Massachusetts men who made at Marietta, in 1788, the initial organized settlement northwest of the Ohio River, are appreciatively and extensively treated in the State chapters with which they are inveterately involved.

But with the Western Reserve the case is quite different. While indisputably the largest of the several distinct elements, or

Preface

colonies, composing Ohio, it was also the latest of the four principal ones, and had a comparatively small part in the original formation of the commonwealth to which it contributed later so largely of men and influence.

A sufficient reason for its specialized treatment is its importance; but its distinctness and strength of individuality also are conducive to this procedure. It was for a long time alluded to because of its radical political character, and, now for its aloofness, again for its aggressiveness, characterized as "a State separate from Ohio," and indeed it was never fully merged until 1860 with that oneness of political opinion in paramount principles to which Ohio then finally attained.

Upon the simple consideration of chronological propriety and because of the initiative of colonial expansion which it afforded, the "Connecticut movement" is here given priority of place; not that in its own history the Western Reserve is earliest, but that its hugely important and inseparable antecedents, without which it is not an understand-

Ohio and Her Western Reserve

able entity, antedate any other portions of the subject of the work.

These causative antecedents have here, for the first time, so far as the author is aware, been presented in their true and compelling connection with the later subject. Their somewhat elaborate presentation, as it here appears, was originally set forth in A Story of Three States, published in the April and May (1902) numbers of Scribner's Magazine, to the proprietors of which, Messrs. Charles Scribner's Sons, the author expresses his gratitude for the privilege of reprinting them.

It may be added that the introductory chapter, outlining Connecticut's history, especially as regards her splendid pioneer services for civil liberty and internal colonial expansion, appears very nearly in the form in which it was delivered as the annual address before the Wyoming Commemorative Association, at Wyoming, Pa., on July 3, 1902. It is here reproduced as exhibiting the inception in the seaboard commonwealth of those ideas and moral and material forces which found their fullest, most significant

Preface

expression in her colony in the old-time West and on the way thither, and which to a considerable extent were formative causes of our national republicanism, our remarkable continental expansion, and our unprecedented prosperity.

THE AUTHOR.

PHILADELPHIA, *October 11, 1902.*

CONTENTS

CHAPTER I
Introductory—Connecticut's service for civil liberty and colonial expansion 3

CHAPTER II
Wyoming, or Connecticut militant in Pennsylvania—The beginnings of "Expansion"—The Yankee invasion and first series of "Pennamite Wars" . . . 53

CHAPTER III
Battle and massacre of Wyoming and flight of survivors through the "Shades of Death" 78

CHAPTER IV
Far-reaching results of war's horror at Wyoming—Ranking with Lexington and Concord in effect on the fortunes of the Revolution—Effort to create a Yankee State in Pennsylvania—Close of "Pennamite Wars" adverse to Connecticut colonists—The Western Reserve as a recompense for Wyoming 101

CHAPTER V
The Western Reserve, or Connecticut triumphant in Ohio—The largest evidence of our organized colonial expansion and the last footprint of Puritanism . . 129

Ohio and Her Western Reserve

CHAPTER VI

PAGE

The Reserve a conservation of Connecticut, yet with differences—The old Puritan idea of liberty comes to the fore in new form—Antislavery a logical outcome of progressive Puritanism—Giddings and Wade, as types of the people and as examples of heredity . . 158

CHAPTER VII

The Reserve's contributions to public service in statesmanship—Literature—Culture—Colleges and public schools—Famous educators—The reflex tide toward Connecticut 190

CHAPTER VIII

Ohio and "the Great Ordinance" of 1787—A huge moral engine operating automatically for the selection of the best elements of immigration—A study of origins 215

CHAPTER IX

Ohio achieves statehood—Gained by the Jeffersonian Democracy in a battle royal with the Federalists and Gen. Arthur St. Clair—Some curious constitutional consequences 236

CHAPTER X

Ohio's ascendency analyzed—An analysis reveals that it was based largely on "selection" of population—The ordinance of freedom massed here Southern as well Northern antislavery forces—A State settled by all the States—Results of the commingling . . . 261

Contents

CHAPTER XI

PAGE

Ohio in the war and in national civil life—Remarkable roster exhibiting the State's prestige—Causes of the latter—Ohioans in literature, journalism, and the arts 279

CHAPTER XII

Summary and conclusion—Causes of political prestige—Ohio's vote—Population—Ohio's immense contribution of population to Western States 307

INDEX 317

LIST OF FULL-PAGE ILLUSTRATIONS

	FACING PAGE
The Ohio Presidents . . . . *Frontispiece*	
The Rev. Thomas Hooker	16
Arrest of the Connecticut settlers	70
"Queen Esther" (Catharine Montour) inciting the Indians to attack Wyoming	88
Flight of the Connecticut settlers through "the Shades of Death"	98
Present aspect of the Wyoming battle-field . . .	104
The Wyoming Monument, erected in 1833 near the scene of battle and massacre	124
How the Connecticut pioneers came into the Western Reserve	129
Fort Harmar, on the Ohio River, at the mouth of the Muskingum, built 1785–'86	215
Campus Martius, first home of the first settlers of Ohio, at Marietta	227
"These are my Jewels"—"Favorite Sons" Monument in Capitol grounds at Columbus	287

MAPS

	PAGE
Lands claimed by Connecticut in Pennsylvania and Ohio	59
The Western Reserve	167

OHIO AND HER WESTERN RESERVE

—But bolder they who first off-cast
Their moorings from the habitable Past,
And ventured chartless on the sea
Of storm-engendering Liberty.
        Lowell.

CHAPTER I

INTRODUCTORY — CONNECTICUT'S SERVICE FOR CIVIL LIBERTY AND COLONIAL EXPANSION

SOMETIMES I have wondered if it is too much to say that Connecticut was the most radical, resistless, and destiny-laden outcome of Puritanism in America. The old Bay State —all honor to her noble history—admittedly excelled her in the production of results greater in totality; but if she was stronger, she was also slower of moral movement—more conservative—than Connecticut. The mother colony lagged behind her eldest daughter in the mental energy of initiative; and, I think, not alone in chronological primacy, but in the vast moment of single acts, was the inferior of her offspring.

Connecticut's, like all early Puritanism, whether we find it in England or on the shores of the new Western world, contained

Ohio and Her Western Reserve

those many rigid, unlovely, and reprehensible doctrines which brought upon the peculiar people the almost universal ridicule of the rest of the world and much of bitter hatred. But the one vast and vital ideal that Puritanism gave to the world, the one doctrine of inestimable value and imperishable influence, not England nor any of her colonies cherished more carefully and zealously, or pushed more persistently into practical usefulness for the advance of mankind than did Connecticut. This was the novel and startling doctrine of human liberty which rose upon the world as a pale, ineffectual star, undistinguishable, save to the keenest vision, from some ephemeral earth light, but growing, glowing, in its slow rise to the meridian, with the life-giving force and the celestial splendor of a sun.

We are too ready to think of Puritanism's seamy side; too prone altogether, save in our most thoughtful and searching moods, to look back upon the Puritan of Old England and of New England as a particularly grim and gloomy Calvinist who ruthlessly renounced everything in life that was joyous and beauti-

Introductory

ful. All of us, and all the time, remember readily enough Macaulay's satirical remark, which smacked more strongly of the sneers made by his Elizabethan predecessors than of the enlightened spirit of his contemporaries of the middle nineteenth century. Yes, we all recall the historian's mot that "the Puritan hated bear-baiting, not because it gave pain to the bear, but because it gave pleasure to the spectators," a witticism, by the way, which Macaulay stole from Hume; but we do not so readily recall that both Macaulay and Hume, in sober earnest, bore testimony to the lofty character of the Puritans and the priceless boon they fairly forced upon a blind and reluctant people in two continents.

Hume, writing of the arbitrary nature of Elizabeth's government, said: "So absolute indeed was the authority of the crown, that the precious spark of liberty had been kindled and was preserved by Puritans alone; and it was to this sect whose principles appear so frivolous and habits so ridiculous, that the English owe the whole freedom of their constitution." And again: "It was only

Ohio and Her Western Reserve

during the next generation that the noble principles of liberty took root, and spreading themselves under the shelter of Puritanical absurdities, became fashionable among the people."

But the truth that Hume told was not recognized even in his time, for he relates in his autobiography that for his utterances he "was assailed by one cry of reproach, disapprobation, and even detestation" from every side and every party, for there was general indignation abroad in the land at the suggestion that English liberty began with the growth of Puritanism. Hallam, though he criticized some of the statements of Hume, practically agreed with him upon the matter we are here concerned with, saying that it was the Puritans who were "the depositaries of the sacred fire" and who "revived the smoldering embers."

Yet it needed a man of the insight, the honesty, the fearlessness, and the sledge-wielding strength of Thomas Carlyle, to first properly characterize the greatest religious, moral, and political force of modern times. He called English Puritanism "the last of all

Introductory

our heroisms." He affirmed that "few nobler heroisms, at bottom, perhaps, no nobler heroism, ever transacted itself on this earth; and it lies as good as lost to us; overwhelmed under such an avalanche of human stupidities as no heroism before ever did. Intrinsically and extrinsically it may be considered inac‚ cessible to these generations. Intrinsically‧ the spiritual purport of it has become inconceivable, incredible to the modern mind. Extrinsically, the documents and records of it, scattered waste as a shoreless chaos, are not legible."

Elsewhere he says: "The resuscitation of a heroism from the past time is no easy enterprise," and then he enters upon and executes it, giving the initiation to others, who in more recent years have gone far beyond him in resuscitating this "last of all our heroisms," and convincing the world that—though it went clothed in an awful and forbidding austerity; though it frowned upon much that was innocent and blithesome and beautiful in life; though it long time fostered hateful and hideous fanaticisms—it was in all verity as noble a heroism "as ever transacted itself on this

Ohio and Her Western Reserve

earth" and that its invincible spirit, in spite of the dross with which it was long laden, gave England constitutional liberty and America political freedom, self-government, and the beginnings of its true democracy.

Having performed these momentous functions Puritanism has such huge items to its credit on the rolls of Clio, that the infinitesimal charges against it, innumerable though they are, and forming a considerable aggregate, fall, by comparison, into nothingness.

To understand to-day the extreme severity of the Puritans' view we must make our comparisons, not with the present, but with the past, and we should very minutely study the conditions, religious, moral, social, and political, that obtained in England when the Puritans' protest was made. Puritanism was born in an age of governmental tyranny, official malfeasance and all-pervading corruption, which logically brought, in due time, a revolution.

The Puritans have been blamed by the superficial for their rejection of the literature of their time. It is true that for the most part they discountenanced and denounced it,

Introductory

but that was because it reflected the evil spirit, the rapacity, the licentiousness, and the reeking rottenness of the age. The great writers of the time cared not a whit for the sacred flame of liberty which lay in the sole guardianship of the Puritans; indeed, they were uniformly and incessantly truculent toward the Puritans and toward the masses in general, while most servilely truckling to the aristocracy.

The Puritans' attitude of aversion, then, to the literature of their time was by no means indicative of intellectual inferiority, but of that uncompromising moral rigidity which made them a mighty force in the movement of civilization.

The name "Puritan" came into the language about 1564, soon after the accession of Elizabeth. From time to time its strict meaning changed, sometimes being used in a religious, sometimes in a political sense. Its popular employment was in a religious sense, and it finally came to have a very liberal application, being extended to all who, either by conduct or word, protested against the irreligion and immorality of the time—in fact, "to

Ohio and Her Western Reserve

pretty nearly everybody who went to church regularly and didn't get drunk." In the strict sense of the appellation it denominated those Calvinistic members of the English Church who would work a reformation from within, while those who left the Church were called Separatists, Independents, Brownists, and the like. To the former class belonged the great majority of the colonists of New England, but it was from the latter that came the Pilgrim fathers who settled in Plymouth, though the majority of the Massachusetts settlers were of the strict Puritan sect; and it was principally from the towns formed by a large influx of this element in 1630 that Connecticut was settled in 1633-'36.

Now Puritanism, though it had set in operation the forces that were most largely instrumental in making modern England, became there in due time an almost inert thing —a frozen creed. The remarkable and momentous fact is, that on the virgin soil of the New World it thawed out, obtained a fresh impetus of life, adapted itself to new conditions, and wrought gradually new wonders, which, after the passing of a century and a

Introductory

half, became the heritage of the whole American people.

In a word, there was engrafted upon Puritanism in America a new idea and a new source of power. Unto Puritanism there was added progressivism. Connecticut was its best and first outcome and exemplar. She led the new advance. It is the popular opinion that no people were less progressive or more stubbornly conservative—"hide-bound" is the vernacular of the condition—than these Puritans. That is unquestionably true of them in a hundred matters—civil, social, and religious; but it is equally true that in the great fundamentals they made early, quickly, and surely, colossal strides beyond all the other colonists of America.

Let us look briefly upon the manner of its doing, and see how and why Connecticut led the vanguard of civilization in its newest and mightiest march.

The passionate love of liberty that constituted the Puritan's predominant trait was the leaven that, little by little, worked its slow way toward its consummation, and evolved from the Connecticut character the

Ohio and Her Western Reserve

greatest of Connecticut achievements. Yet this was not accomplished through a simple process. It was complicated—inveterately interwoven, one may say—with the Puritan's religion. The settlement of Connecticut and her early service for freedom, for self-government, for democracy, and ultimately for nationality, could not conceivably have come about save for the fact that Puritan local government went hand in hand with religion.

To the now execrated "union of Church and state," on a miniature scale, we owe in part, at least, the remarkable progressivism with which Connecticut imbued Puritanism. The "town" and the church were practically one. It followed naturally—and it was a frequent occurrence, among a people who had learned as no English-speaking people before had done, to think and act for themselves—that when schism arose in the church the dissenting minority, firm in their conviction of right, and unwilling to be coerced, moved out and onward, and established a "town" and church of their own.

Sometimes the incentive arose from the regard for political rather than religious free-

Introductory

dom. But in either case the result was the same. The seceders were naturally in moral advance of those whom they left, and thus it happened that each exodus from Massachusetts into Connecticut planted in the latter State some of the choicest souls from the older colony. If Massachusetts "was sown with selected grain," as has been truthfully enough claimed, Connecticut was sown with twice-winnowed grain.

Thus conscience, courage, love of religious and civil liberty, in their influence upon character (already made individually independent and self-reliant by the very conditions under which the pioneer Puritans of New England lived), performed automatically, as it were, a kind of silent, but incessant, and enormously effective work of selection for the building up of Connecticut, and her moral equipment for that sublime service in which she took the bold initiative.

The settlement of 1633, the first lawful, organized English occupation of Connecticut, was made by a little party of the dissatisfied from Plymouth. They founded Windsor. It was shortly after that another company from

Ohio and Her Western Reserve

Massachusetts settled Wethersfield, and in 1636 a much larger party founded Hartford. In the last-mentioned year a desire for a more democratic form of government caused a considerable exodus from the mother colony, and all three of these towns then received their chief bodies of immigrants.

It was of immense importance that at this juncture there came to Hartford one Thomas Hooker, an English clergyman, driven

GRAVE OF THOMAS HOOKER, IN CENTER CHURCH CEMETERY, HARTFORD, CONN.

The inscription reads: "In memory of the Rev. Thomas Hooker, who in 1636 with his assistant Mr. Stone removed to Hartford with about 100 persons, where he planted the first Church in Connecticut. An eloquent, able, and faithful Minister of Christ. He died July 7th, 1647. ÆT. LXI."

from his native land for non-conformity, a resident of Holland from 1630 to 1633, then a settler of Boston, and finally, after three

Introductory

years there, being dissatisfied with the illiberal spirit that prevailed, leading into the wilderness the broader-minded men who were willingly his followers, and among whom, in their new home, he planted and nourished the fundamental thought that was formulated in an instrument on January 14, 1639, and adopted by the three towns thus compacted in a body politic. This was the first written constitution known to history, with the possible exception of the "Union of Utrecht," under which the Netherlands were then living, and which it is permissible to call a constitution, and it was absolutely the "first in America to embody the democratic idea."

It is a popular fallacy that democracy dawned upon America in the compact made on the Mayflower—a compact that opened with a formal acknowledgment of the king as the source of all authority, and which contained no new political principle and no suggestion of democracy or liberty whatever. Such democracy as Massachusetts had in its early days was in reality accidental, and not institutional, while that of Connecticut was created consciously and deliberately; and the

Ohio and Her Western Reserve

true democracy, to which the Bay State afterward became so splendidly devoted, she owed chiefly to the example set by her eldest daughter, Connecticut.

There is now no question of Hooker's authorship, at least of the idea, of this remarkable document of 1639. An abstract of a sermon that he delivered in 1638, seven months before the constitution was signed, has been discovered in very recent years, which puts the preacher's claim upon an impregnable basis. He spoke from the text, Deuteronomy i, 13–15 : "Take you wise men, and understanding and known among your tribes, and I will make them rulers over you ... captains over thousands, and captains over hundreds, over fifties, over tens," etc. ; and with this as his basis, he pointed out "that the choice of public magistrates belongs unto the people, by God's own allowance ; that the privilege of election, which belongs to the people, must not be exercised according to their humors, but according to the blessed will and law of God ; that they who have power to appoint officers and magistrates, it is in their power, also, to set the bounds and

THE REV. THOMAS HOOKER, PURITAN PREACHER (1586–1647).

No authentic portrait of Thomas Hooker exists, but Niehaus's statue in the Connecticut Capitol is a carefully made composite based upon the likenesses of various members of his lineal posterity and historical description.

Introductory

limitations of the power and place to which they call them; because (1) the foundation of authority is laid, firstly, in the free consent of the people; because (2) by a free choice, the hearts of the people will be more inclined to the love of the persons chosen and more readily lend obedience."

Finally, the Puritan preacher spoke of the "uses" of the text and the doctrine he deduced from it, being such as "to persuade us, as God hath given us liberty, *to take it*," and "as God hath spared our lives, and given us them in liberty, so to seek the guidance of God, and to choose in God and for God."

Herein, at Hartford, was lain down the germinal idea of political liberty for the individual, the beginning of democracy, and the corner-stone, at least, of that foundation on which the firm fabric of the American commonwealth was slowly upreared. Herein was the first practical assertion of the right of the people not only to choose, but to limit the powers of their rulers. There was neither in the inspiring sermon of liberty-loving Thomas Hooker nor in the constitution based upon it, any allusion to a "dread sovereign"

Ohio and Her Western Reserve

nor any expression of deference to class. Sermon and constitution were alike instinct with liberty and democracy.

It may seem like a little thing that was gained on the banks of the Connecticut in 1638 and 1639 when we compare it with the civil liberty we now enjoy, but the true historical methods of estimate is to compare every movement of advance with what existed before, and not with what came after, and thus viewed the Connecticut Puritan declaration of rights of a quarter of a millennial since, in the very infancy of the colonies, was a giant stride in the history of human liberty.

The constitution, says one of the State historians, provided "a system of complete popular control, of frequent elections by the people, and of minute local government," and it remained throughout the confiscations, modifications, and refusals of charters in other colonies the exemplar of the rights of self-government, which all colonies gradually came to aim at more or less consciously.

A brief glance at some of the other enactments with which these Puritans benefited

Introductory

the whole people, and we have done with Connecticut achievement in this line, and pass to the consideration of other forms of her evolutionary force. First of all, she legalized, by the famous constitution of 1639, the written ballot, in a form introduced by Hooker, which was a great improvement upon that adopted in Massachusetts; and, unlike some of the other colonies, kept it in perpetual use until it was fixed as an integral part of the political system of the nation. She established and maintained the "town" system on a basis even more independent of outside control than that of Massachusetts, making it emphatically the unit of political organizations, which, because it came nearest to the people, won the recognition of Tocqueville as a leading factor in true democratic government. More, too, than Massachusetts she was influential in passing this invaluable institution to the West, where it perpetuated many of her principles, and became a potent cause of the political supremacy of the regions to which it was carried.

Connecticut by this same famous first constitution practically indorsed Massachu-

Ohio and Her Western Reserve

setts's educational system, but exceeded the mother colony in the strenuousness of its advocacy, and made those towns which should fail to maintain free schools subject to fine.

Finally, when the Constitution of the United States was formed, through the peculiar position her delegates held in the convention and by adroit management, she was enabled to incorporate in it that measure for the benefit of the small States which gave equality of representation in the upper house of Congress and a proportional representation in the lower—a measure which was derived directly from her own system of town representation established in 1639.

Even when apparently stationary, Connecticut was constantly moving forward— a pioneer in the lines of human liberty and political righteousness—moving forward mightily, though invisibly, in thought, until she was ready for the conspicuity of vigorous action, for she was constantly recruited by the most advanced men of less liberal Massachusetts and of England.

We have said that Connecticut's signal service to humanity along the pathway of

Introductory

liberty lay in her adding progressivism to Puritanism. Many instances have been cited. There remains one which all cavillers at Connecticut's alleged conservatism should bear in mind. In 1650, twelve years before the union of Connecticut and the New Haven colony, both colonies, which had similar laws, reduced the number of crimes for which capital punishment was inflicted from 160 to 15 —the number remaining formidable enough, in all conscience. But let us look at that England from which these Puritans had migrated. As late as 1819, over a century and a half after her American offspring's action, we find that she carried no less than 223 capital offenses upon her code. No commentary is needed, one may think, upon this indication of the comparative advance of humanity in Old and in New England.

The whole of this wonderful achievement under the Connecticut Puritan constitution of 1639, and a vast deal more that we can not specify within our limitations, was the outgrowth of the ever-evolving idea of liberty, constantly quickened and fostered to early fruition in Connecticut by the peculiar con-

Ohio and Her Western Reserve

ditions in Massachusetts that the radical, conscienceful character of some of her people could not comply with. Massachusetts's illiberality continuously acted as an expulsive force upon some of her foremost men, and certainly her most progressive minds, and thus built up the more progressive Puritanism of her neighbor.

Glancing swiftly over the field and across the years, it would seem as if, in the language of modern science, an immense idea evolved through the minds of Puritan Thomas Hooker and his Connecticut followers, as the vital principle evolves through protoplasm, to form a new order of life. But if, instead of the cold locution of science, we employ the reverent language which the Puritan himself might use, when we think of what the Connecticut colonists did for liberty in those early years, and coming down to the later ones, contemplate their descendants, as we shall, when they fought for liberty in 1776, and still later made the idea of liberty apply to the abolition of black slavery, by moral agitation in the '30s, '40s, and '50s, and by martial action in the '60s—if, as I say, thinking of

Introductory

all this, and of Connecticut men in Connecticut, joined by Connecticut men in Pennsylvania and in the Western Reserve, heroically urging and soundly legislating for the propaganda of freedom, we should say, even as the Puritan himself would say, that in the larger affairs of men and nations—as in the raising up of Oliver Cromwell and of Abraham Lincoln—the hand of God in some mysterious manner reaches directly down to humanity and impels mankind forward in the march of destiny.

Let us turn now to another line of Connecticut achievement, in which every episode flowing, like those already considered, from the fondly cherished idea of liberty, but influenced also by varied moral and material conditions, in some degree reacted upon, modified, and remolded the original Connecticut Puritan character in which they had their inception. The reference here made is, of course, to that altogether remarkable and unparalleled colonial expansion of Connecticut which had its origin in the middle of the eighteenth century, upon the ground since

Ohio and Her Western Reserve

made historic as Wyoming—the true Windsor of the West—where heroic blood dyed the Susquehanna in the same progressive cause of liberty that had its first announcement on the Connecticut.

The great westward pressure of Connecticut was in a measure resultant from the same forces that governed the settlement of Connecticut itself—that is, church secession and the desire for a more democratic government, both elements in the passion for freedom. But material conditions also entered into the complex cause of the exodus.

As early as 1680, when Connecticut had already sent offshoots of population into New Jersey and lower Pennsylvania, as well as into some contiguous territory, the colonial government, in obeying a request from England for a statement of its condition, responded through a letter in the hand of John Allyn, stating, among other things, that the country was mountainous, full of rocks, swamps, hills, and vales; that most of it that was fit for planting had been taken up; and that "what remaynes must be subdued and gained out of the fire, as it were, by hard

Introductory

blowes and for small recompence." If this was the truth in regard to the then existing condition in Connecticut, it was no less a correct prophecy of what was awaiting the settlers at Wyoming a century later. To subdue and to gain "out of the fire, by hard blowes and for small recompence," was indeed the usual lot of the Puritan in Connecticut and the Puritan patriot in Pennsylvania. It was to this circumstance that was attributable the development of a very unusual spirit of enterprise and an indomitable courageousness in a character already well equipped with other sterling virtues.

Now Connecticut, which had when Allyn wrote his description in 1680 a population of only 10,000 to 12,000 souls, and was poor in property, though rich in the quality of its men, weak in actual fighting strength, though strong in the stout hearts and independence of its people (as was shown half a dozen years later by their secreting the royal grant of their colony in the Charter Oak rather than surrendering it to the British Government), grew steadily, though slowly, in population. Trumbull estimates its people at

Ohio and Her Western Reserve

17,000 in 1713, and the Board of Trade at 100,000 and Bancroft at 133,000 in 1755. At the latter date older and larger Massachusetts is estimated to have had 207,000, and vast Virginia only 168,000 population.

Thus it will be seen Connecticut held no mean position in the group of colonies. In proportion to its territory, it was perhaps the most populous of all of them, and long before 1762, when all of the soil had been allotted into towns, the people had manifested a disposition to swarm from a hive that seemed to them too small to accommodate their liberal views of life.

The Delaware Company was first in the field with its settlement at Cushutunk in 1757, and the Susquehanna Company followed in 1762, after the close of the Indian War. Pennsylvania, but for the blind or misconceiving policy of its people, largely influenced by the interested proprietaries, might have had as a result of this settlement as large an influx of the best population in America as Ohio afterward received. But an indiscriminate and incessant opposition deprived the very State which most

Introductory

particularly needed it of nine-tenths of the body which would probably have come on conditions of fair terms and friendliness.

One result of this deflection of immigration was exhibited in the founding of a settlement of Connecticut men in the far South, which has been generally neglected by Connecticut historians. This was the settlement in 1776 (projected at Hartford in 1772) of Natchez, Miss. (then included in West Florida), made by several hundred New England families, mostly from Connecticut. There were some among these people who scantily sympathized with the political revolt in New England, but Justin Winsor has said: "There was enough, however, of the Revolutionary fervor of the Atlantic seaboard in others to make the settlement an important factor in shaping the destiny of this Southern region." And we deem it eminently deserving of a place in the list of Connecticut's achievements in the line of colonization.

If Wyoming was the settlement made and maintained under the most strenuous exertions and heroic sacrifice, almost literally

Ohio and Her Western Reserve

"subdued and gained out of the fire by hard blowes and for small recompence," the Western Reserve in Ohio was the settlement made most easefully and successfully—absolutely without any expenditure of blood within its limits—and most fully and continuously stood as an expositor in the West of all that was admirable in Connecticut.

But we must not forget that Wyoming, so to speak, sounded the inspiring music and set the pace for the westward march; that Wyoming really influenced the settlement of a great number of Connecticut men in other parts of Pennsylvania than by the Susquehanna's waters; and last, but not least, that the blood of the Wyoming martyrs, shed a century and a quarter ago, in reality paid the unnamed price for the Connecticut Western Reserve.

Nor must we fail to recognize the importance of those unorganized and scattering settlements with which Connecticut dotted Vermont and western New York, southern Michigan, northern Indiana and Illinois, Iowa and Kansas, and even California and the Pacific Slope. Further let us bear in mind that it

Introductory

was Moses Austin, a Connecticut man temporarily settled in Missouri, who conceived and his son, Stephen F. Austin, who executed a considerable scheme for the "Americanization" of far-off Texas, and in the second decade of the last century diverted from the natural westward course a sufficient number of mixed Connecticut and Missouri men to found auspiciously the flourishing city of Austin. Thus we see that while Connecticut, like a mighty vine, shot its main stem 600 miles westward, stanch and strong, through three States — Pennsylvania, New York, and Ohio—the tendrils, so to speak, of that vine touched the widely remote shores of the great Gulf and the Golden Gate.

It is to this wide dispersion of Connecticut men, caused by the discontent with the conditions in the old colony which their own progressivism gave birth to, and to the predominance of capacity and energy in their characters that we must ascribe the influence of Connecticut in the affairs of other States and in the nation and the great number of individual Connecticut men who rose to positions of honorable conspicuity in the

Ohio and Her Western Reserve

middle region of the West. One historian says that as early as 1857 the single county of Litchfield was noted as the birthplace of thirteen United States senators, twenty-two representatives from New York, fifteen Supreme Court judges in other States, nine presidents of colleges and eighteen other professors, and eleven governors and lieutenant-governors of States. If we were to attempt a similar list for the whole State and bring it down to the present time, we should find that it would contain thousands of names of men eminent in public life from Chief Executives down to congressmen.

One can appreciate the feelings of the inquiring foreigner who hearing constantly that this or that great man, though a resident of Pennsylvania, or Ohio, or New York, was born in Connecticut, went to the atlas to look up the wonderful region that was so prolific of men of power, and was most wofully disappointed to find that Connecticut, after all, was "nothing but a little green spot on the map."

Another notable effect of the whole westward movement from Connecticut was that upon the men who took part in it. While

Introductory

in the original colony progressive liberalism in civil and religious thought moved by inches, we find—whether it was owing to some subtle alchemy in the aroma of the new soil and of the wild wood, or to the simple fact that those who became pioneers were naturally more advanced than their stay-at-home contemporaries—that progress was made by leaps and bounds, surpassing all precedent. Particularly was this true in the outward aspect of religion. Formality to a great extent was relinquished.

In the first settlement of Ohio, made at Marietta, principally by Massachusetts men, we find that the unnatural and awe-compelling dignity of the New England clergyman had so far fallen from him, that he run a foot-race on the Fourth of July and distanced his competitor, a lawyer, a circumstance that the local poet preserved in the allusion:—

>It was a fact, they all gave in,
>Divinity could outstrip Sin.

And there was a similar relaxation of sacerdotal severity with similar retention of power to triumph over sin in Wyoming and the Western Reserve.

Ohio and Her Western Reserve

The probability is that the Yankee idea, long growing, though unobserved, the qualities of thriftiness and shrewdness under the hard conditions, and the increasing competition for livelihood in Connecticut, had finally added a beneficial practicality to progressive Puritanism. And did not this practicality include an advance in that commercial capability for which this people became noted? At any rate, it is safe to say that the Connecticut Yankee in the West evinced with surprising unanimity and certitude that if he conformed his life to the exhortation "Be thou fervent in spirit; not slothful in business; serving the Lord," he regarded the second clause of the injunction as equally with the first and the final one calling for his obedience.

The general statement is true that Congregationalism, which had in 1742 been made the established religion in Connecticut, was within the old colony, and even in the mother State, a kind of congealed creed, containing much of the *débris* of an effete Calvinism, with the cold purity that formed its really majestic mass; but in the frontier set-

Introductory

tlements much of the former was liberated by a general melting process. The Yankee in his new homes engrafted practicality upon his religion as he did upon all things, and gradually the amenities and humanities of a wholesome life displaced the asperities and austerities of Calvinism without any noticeable abatement of the splendid moral force that had originally moved the people with the idea of liberty.

Indeed a deep reverence for religion was the prevalent characteristic of the Western settlements of Connecticut, and, combined with the passion for education which everywhere reared free schools among the forest homes; with the political vantage inherent in the operation of the "town meeting"; and the federative idea, which was the foundation of democracy, constituted Connecticut's best benefaction to the always advancing borderland of civilization, which, in turn, was to grow old and pass its influence onward to the younger West.

Connecticut's contributions to the cause of education, to the material progress of the

Ohio and Her Western Reserve

country, to invention, and to manufacture, great as they were, we must pass with a word, but in viewing Connecticut's achievement as the outcome of Connecticut character, we can not fail to dwell upon the wars in which the Yankee Puritan fought for that same freedom, in advanced form, for which he had thought and wrought with patient persistence from the dawn of the primitive idea of liberty and its declaration in the constitution of 1639.

Passing over the French and Indian War, in which the men of Connecticut performed a large service and gained fighting experience which served them well in the later and greater struggle, we find, naturally enough, that in the Revolution, more than in any former exigency which Connecticut faced, she exhibited that judicial consideration, combined with conscience, which renders people strong in the execution of an enterprise once carefully weighed and undertaken.

Religion was a strong factor in the war achievements of the colony and the State. The righteousness of opposition to the Eng-

Introductory

lish government was tried by standards of an orthodox, but evolutionary, Puritanism in every pulpit in Connecticut, and most deliberately and earnestly discussed by the laymen of every community. It was true, as Macaulay said, that the Puritan "brought to civil and military affairs a coolness of judgment and an immutability of purpose which some writers have thought inconsistent with religious zeal, but which were in fact the necessary effects of it."

It was characteristic of the Connecticut Puritan to insist upon being right before he went ahead, and his persistency in all endeavors and success in most of them was largely due to his determination to be sure of the sagaciousness, practicability, and the moral legality of an object before bending to its service his really terrible tenacity of purpose. A very curious and interesting item of the secret history of the Revolutionary movement in Connecticut may be cited in illustration of this truth. When the contest was drawing on, the governor called a secret session of the legislature, which on assembling appointed six of the leading jurists of

Ohio and Her Western Reserve

the colony—three to argue the cause in favor of the right of Parliament to tax the colonies, and three against it. These arguments were continued through long sittings for two or three days, when the conviction became universal among the members that the parliamentary right did not exist, and that the colonies might therefore lawfully resist.

Thereupon the question of right being decided and a judicial estimate of the prospect of success assuring the people that the cause was no longer Quixotic or chimerical, the Connecticut Puritans having hitherto exercised a prudent self-restraint under every provocation, abandoned themselves unreservedly to action.

How sagacious, efficient, pertinacious, and heroic that deliberate action was, the lives of Connecticut's most illustrious patriots and

Introductory

the prosaic but proved statistics of history abundantly tell.

Connecticut had as her first "war governor" Jonathan Trumbull, one of the leading friends and most valued counselors of the commander-in-chief—the man to whom Washington's familiar mode of address was "Brother Jonathan"—the original of the personified typical American in our vernacular. She had her signer of the Declaration, Samuel Huntington, who was also President of the Continental Congress; and she had wise counselors and legislators by scores and hundreds, and in the field such men as Israel Putnam, David Wooster, Joseph Spencer, Ethan Allen, Nathan Hale, Wolcott, Knowlton, Grosvenor, Meigs, Huntington, Humphreys, Sears, and Douglas—and also, it must candidly be said, Benedict Arnold! who though a native, Connecticut historians and orators have carefully, on all occasions, shown to have been of Rhode Island descent and commissioned by Massachusetts!

Connecticut was instant in action and unremitting in vigilance and vigor throughout the war, sagaciously aggressive and un-

Ohio and Her Western Reserve

selfishly patriotic, as an early instance of which we have her effective offensive movement against Ticonderoga for the relief of Massachusetts, when she was not herself assailed nor in imminent danger. This was planned in Connecticut and supported from her public treasury before the Continental Congress in 1775 had assembled, and "before the blood had grown cold that was shed at Concord and at Lexington."

Although the principal theater of the war was outside the State, Connecticut contributed most magnificently to its prosecution in men and money, and at one time one-half of Washington's army in the operations about, and the defense of New York was composed of her sons. But the totals of troops furnished by the several colonies tells most compactly and convincingly the story of Connecticut's intense patriotism and of her burning passion for political freedom. She sent into the field 31,959 officers and men, including large detachments from her Wyoming settlements, being second only to Massachusetts (inclusive of Maine), with more than twice her population; largely ex-

Introductory

ceeding Pennsylvania, which had nearly twice as many people; still further exceeding the contribution of Virginia, which had more than three times her population, and almost doubling that of the really more numerically powerful New York.

It was peculiarly characteristic of Connecticut that at first almost wholly, and all through the war to a considerable extent, the measures for organizing and putting the soldiery in the field and for sustaining the army were enacted by the "towns." Almost equally was this condition true nearly a hundred years later when that other conflict came on in 1861, in which the descendants of those who had fought to preserve liberty and create a nation battled with the same valor, though in greatly augmented numbers, to preserve that nation from destruction.

Sam^{el} Huntington

As a State, Connecticut could not at once

Ohio and Her Western Reserve

furnish the single regiment of militia for which the General Government called. The Commonwealth was met by an emergency unprovided for by law, but the patriotic people were not disturbed in the least, and fell back upon the resources of the "town" system, precisely as they would have done two centuries before, and had done in the Revolution.

Governor William A. Buckingham, one of the galaxy of great "war governors," who was to Connecticut in the war of the rebellion very much what Trumbull was during the Revolution, it is true, usurped power in calling for troops, for he was full of faith that the people, through the Assembly, would vindicate him, as they did; but the actual agitation for volunteering and the intense activity entered into for the contribution of funds was carried on by the "towns." And they bore—and some still bear, I believe, to this day—the burden of the debts they so readily and resolutely incurred.

That the management of war affairs was thoroughly effective is evidenced by the fact that a population containing in 1861 only

Introductory

80,000 voters and about 50,000 able-bodied men put into the service of the Union, in all its branches, 54,882 volunteers of all terms of service; or, if the terms are all reduced to a three years' average, over 48,000, exceeding the quota by between six and seven thousand. If the percentage of volunteers was very high—excelled, indeed, by only one or two States—the character and efficiency of Connecticut's troops were surpassed by those of no other State.

Her rosters were filled by men to an unusual degree typical of the best strains of blood in the State and of those who had helped to make its proud history. Theodore Winthrop, the first of Connecticut's sons to fall upon the field, was descended from Puritan John Winthrop, the first governor of Connecticut. Ellsworth, Ward, and Lyon, those other early martyrs of the war, were all of Connecticut stock.

One has only to recall the names of the Connecticut generals and other officials to be reminded of the earlier history of the colony, and to be convinced that the Puritan families, like Puritan principles, were still alive and

Ohio and Her Western Reserve

active. To the navy Connecticut contributed its Secretary Gideon Welles, Rear-admirals Andrew H. Foote and F. H. Gregory, and Commodores John and C. R. P. Rogers and R. B. Hitchcock. In the army her major-generals were Darius N. Couch, Henry W. Benham, John Sedgwick, Alfred H. Terry, J. K. F. Mansfield, Joseph A. Mower, Joseph Hawley, H. W. Birge, Henry L. Abbott, Alexander Shaler, Joseph G. Totten, Henry W. Wessels, A. S. Williams, Horatio G. Wright, and R. O. Tyler; while among the brigadiers were Nathaniel Lyon, O. S. Ferry, Daniel Tyler, Edward Harland, Luther P. Bradley, Henry B. Carrington, William T. Clark, Henry M. Judah, William S. Ketchum, R. S. Mackenzie, James W. Ripley, Benjamin S. Roberts, Truman Seymour, H. D. Terry, and A. von Steinwehr.

If we look below these illustrious men we shall find many more Connecticut men of capacity and heroism, and the rank and file of her soldiery, largely descendants of the Puritans, and all as invincible as Cromwell's Ironsides. If we look, on the other hand, far above the roster of Connecticut's

Introductory

officers we have named, and take into consideration not alone the old Connecticut but the New, and the sterling strains of blood which Connecticut pioneers had carried into Pennsylvania, Ohio, and the farther West—if we let our view comprehend not alone the native-born, but the descendants of Connecticut stock—we shall discover, indeed, a greater and more glorious galaxy of generals and commanders in our latest war for liberty. And most lustrous of the stars in that ever-shining galaxy we shall see two men whom we
may call grandsons of Connecticut—one near the war's close leading that herculean, historic march from Atlanta to the sea; the other, greatest of all, holding Lee in his inexorable grasp upon the James, and finally receiving magnanimously his surrender at Appomattox.

All of this—and more—must have its place in history's sum total of Connecticut

Ohio and Her Western Reserve

achievement, growing logically out of Connecticut character.

And yet the people of the Commonwealth, and those descended from them in Wyoming, in New York, and in the Western Reserve, were far from being a people who placed a high estimate upon strictly soldierly glory. Theirs was always the moral rather than the martial idea. They had, in fact, a positive aversion to war. They must first have a cause for which to fight, and know that cause to be founded on immutable justice.

'Tis true, something of soldierly submission to discipline, of soldierly hardihood, and indifference to death when they were once embattled—qualities beaten into some of their ancestors by the iron hand of Cromwell—may have descended to them; but far more powerful a factor in forming their fighting strength—indeed, almost the supreme influence to which they were susceptible—was that which flowed from devotion to fixed principle, the impassioned love of liberty, and the deep-seated Puritanical conviction that they must follow whithersoever duty led.

Introductory

As the mind of the honest man studying history goes back of Cromwell's time to the beginning of English Puritanism and the birth of civil liberty, and takes a sweeping view downward through three centuries, he can not conceive of the outcome of Connecticut achievement as being wrought by any power other than that of its vigorously progressive and adaptive Puritanism —an absolutely new, virile religious idea, practically applied to and controlling man's conduct in every‧day life, and especially inculcating the doctrine of the right to liberty.

As we glance along the opening years of Connecticut's Puritan history—so poor, so sparse in many of the elements that appeal to and fascinate the superficial and the lover of the merely romantic—we see a figure, plain, prosaic, with a face perchance not comely in the world's way, and we hear a voice, possibly in the despised and ridiculed nasal tone; but the figure rises, looms upward, the face lights and glows with the inspiration of a great idea for the benefit of humanity, present and to come; and the voice, even if nasal, takes on a triumphant, trumpet tone that rings across the centuries.

The figure and the face and the voice are those of Thomas Hooker, Puritan preacher of Connecticut, 1638. And the voice proclaims: "And, lastly, as God hath given us liberty, let us take it"—an utterance more momentous, more pregnant of mighty result, than the mouthings of a host of puppet kings and the deeds of 10,000 melodramatic heroes who may vainly have imagined they were making history. His hearers, exalted, impassioned, by the plain preacher's exhortations, do indeed take, in their constitution of 1639, just a little of that liberty which he has implored them to seize—so pitifully little, it now seems, though large for the time—and democracy and freedom have their beginning on the American continent.

Almost a century and a half later, the descendants of Thomas Hooker's hearers, and others of their kind, take vastly more of man's heritage of liberty—for the Revolution is truly a Puritan measure in inception, if not

Introductory

in execution—and now the splendid spirit of freedom is abroad in the land.

Almost another century glides slowly into the immutable past, and now the idea of liberty takes to itself, under the tutelage of a revived and vivified progressive Puritanism, a new and wondrous form. It has long been a blessing to its possessors, and now becomes a boon which it is their imperative duty to extend to an alien race. We hear the advanced doctrine preached by Charles B. Storrs, a Connecticut man of the Western Reserve; thundered in the nation's Capitol by Wade and Giddings; and helped on its slow way by the "Proviso" of Wilmot, a Connecticut man of Pennsylvania; and after many years there is warfare in which the descendants of Thomas Hooker's hearers and their Connecticut brothers, East and West, take up the gage of battle, not for martial glory, but for the cause of freedom and the preservation of an imperiled Union, fought for and founded on the ground of human liberty by their forefathers.

Liberty is no longer a little thing for some favored few to enjoy, but, "subdued and

Ohio and Her Western Reserve

gained out of the fire by hard blows"—even as was the land and sustenance of the Connecticut Puritan—it has become an inestimable right to be given to all men and to cover the width of the Western world.

It is the new and legitimate projection of an old idea that the sons of the Connecticut colonists are fighting for, and they are actuated, as were their forefathers, by the quick and stern conscience of the Puritan, that knows no flinching when once it has deliberately devoted itself to duty. Religious conviction and patriotism with him, as of old, go hand in hand in the Puritan character, and thus, by dual influence, contribute to the glorious culmination and crown of Connecticut achievement.

For the progressive Puritan, whether of the Commonwealth or its colonies, is profoundly moved by the solemn spirit and heroic resolution which has been formulated in a strophe of reverent and patriotic poetry by a woman of Puritan ancestry, and he goes sternly forth to battle consecrating himself to liberty, even as did Cromwell's soldiers, while the still, small voice of conscience is sound-

Introductory

ing in his soul the majestic import, if not the words:

In the beauty of the lilies Christ was born across the sea,
With a glory in his bosom that transfigures you and me;
As he died to make men holy, let us die to make men free.

Through a long warfare rude,
With patient hardihood,
By toil, and strife, and blood,
The soil was won.
LEWIS J. CIST.

CHAPTER II

WYOMING; OR, CONNECTICUT MILITANT IN PENNSYLVANIA

IF we attempt to follow in detail the sequence of events constituting the most marked of Connecticut's achievements in the material line—her prodigious pioneering in the work of the organized colonization of the West— we shall find that it develops a strange, true, thrilling story of three States, and that ultimately this story reveals the persistence of the moral idea of civil liberty and human freedom to which, as we have seen, Connecticut gave the initiative in her constitution of 1639.

It is purposed to relate in this story the really astounding expansion of Connecticut in the eighteenth century, and the most remarkable movement of internal colonization in the whole history of the country. It will

Ohio and Her Western Reserve

be found the story of Connecticut militant in Pennsylvania, and of Connecticut triumphant in Ohio; of long warfare at Wyoming, and peaceful conquest in the Western Reserve. The beginning of Connecticut's bold bodily projection westward, six hundred miles into the wilderness, was Cushutunk, on the Delaware; and its end—so far as it is definitely marked—is Cleveland, on Lake Erie, now become the chief city of Ohio, and the "Reserve" lying round about it, peopled by that expansive movement of Connecticut, as large, as populous, almost as characteristically Connecticut as is the mother State.

Who ever heard of Cushutunk? Who has not heard of Cleveland? They were the products of one and the same force. Of the half-century of time and the strange warfare in the wilderness that lay between them, and of the final vicarious reward of victory in Ohio, this story tells.

Cushutunk's humble being was begun on a soft day in June, 1757, when the solitude and solemn quiet of the valley of the upper Delaware were rudely broken by the resounding strokes of axes sturdily swung—

Wyoming

always the first signal of the forest conquerors' coming—and a cluster of rude log cabins arose in the tiny niche which a band of Connecticut pioneers had chopped in the wall of fresh foliage on the western bank of the river, far up toward the north line of Pennsylvania. Penn's province was well settled to the southward, but all west of this handful of adventurers was a wilderness, clear to the setting sun. It was only a minute dot of civilization which these "Yankees" placed in the present county of Wayne, in Penn's dominion, and some five years later, when Wyoming was planted, it had but thirty families; but it involved most momentous issues.

It was the first, the pioneer settlement of the Connecticut people within the boundaries of Penn's province. It represented the first overt act of an intercolonial intrusion; the initial movement of that persistent, general, systematic invasion which resulted in the settlement of Wyoming and the establishment of a Connecticut colony and a Connecticut government on Pennsylvania soil; a determined effort to dismember the State and

Ohio and Her Western Reserve

to create another, to be carved from the territory of Pennsylvania; and all of the varied acts, the dissension and strife, armed conflict and frequent bloodshed of what have been commonly called the "Pennamite Wars." But beyond these effects, the action of the "Yankee" invaders of a coveted land, to which they believed themselves rightly entitled, became inextricably interwoven in cause and consequence with that darkest deed of the border warfare of the Revolution, the bloody massacre of Wyoming. This, in turn, had a marked effect in England in creating sympathy for the colonies. The fame of Wyoming went far abroad, but the effects of the movement, of which the massacre was an episode, became immensely important at home. The half-century of contention opened with the Yankee invasion proved almost too much for colonial ability to adjust; and it became an embarrassing legacy to the young Union, which it was feared by many prudent patriots might demonstrate a fatal weakness in its cohesive quality. It was amicably settled, however, in a way which not only avoided disaster but helped to cement the

Wyoming

confederation; and when the long lingering clouds of the Pennamite Wars had been finally dispersed, it was found that the practical results of Connecticut's persistent colonization project had been the incorporation of a small but beneficial element of Yankee blood in the body politic of Pennsylvania; and, on the part of Connecticut, the proud possession of what equaled a State—more than ten times as much ground as she had fought for in Pennsylvania—but beyond her borders, in that then No Man's Land, the old Northwest Territory by the shore of Lake Erie, the famous "Western Reserve," in the future State of Ohio. And thus, after long tribulations, ended in triumph the strangest and most strenuous organized movement in the whole history of Western colonization.

So much, in brief, for the Omega of the movement, which had its tangible Alpha at old Cushutunk, on the Delaware.

Cushutunk and Wyoming were established under the auspices of two separate companies organized in Connecticut, and actuated by a common purpose — the colonization of the westward-lying lands covered by Connecti-

Ohio and Her Western Reserve

cut's charter—in other words, northern Pennsylvania. Wyoming was founded by what was known as the Connecticut Susquehanna Company, and Cushutunk by the Delaware Company. Both had precisely the same basis of claim, and both sought to attain their ends by precisely the same methods, but the Susquehanna Company, because the stronger, became prominent in history, while the Delaware Company was left in comparative obscurity.

All this contention about the possession of a part of the Quaker province with its far-reaching consequences, it will be recalled, had its origin in the ignorance and indifference of the British monarchs concerning American geography and the confusion that ensued from carelessness in the granting of royal charters to the several colonies. Several of them overlapped, and thus caused conflicts of authority in regard to ownership.

Connecticut's charter, which was granted by Charles II in 1662, confirming and combining former charters and deeds, conveyed to that colony all of the territory of the present State, *and all of the lands west of*

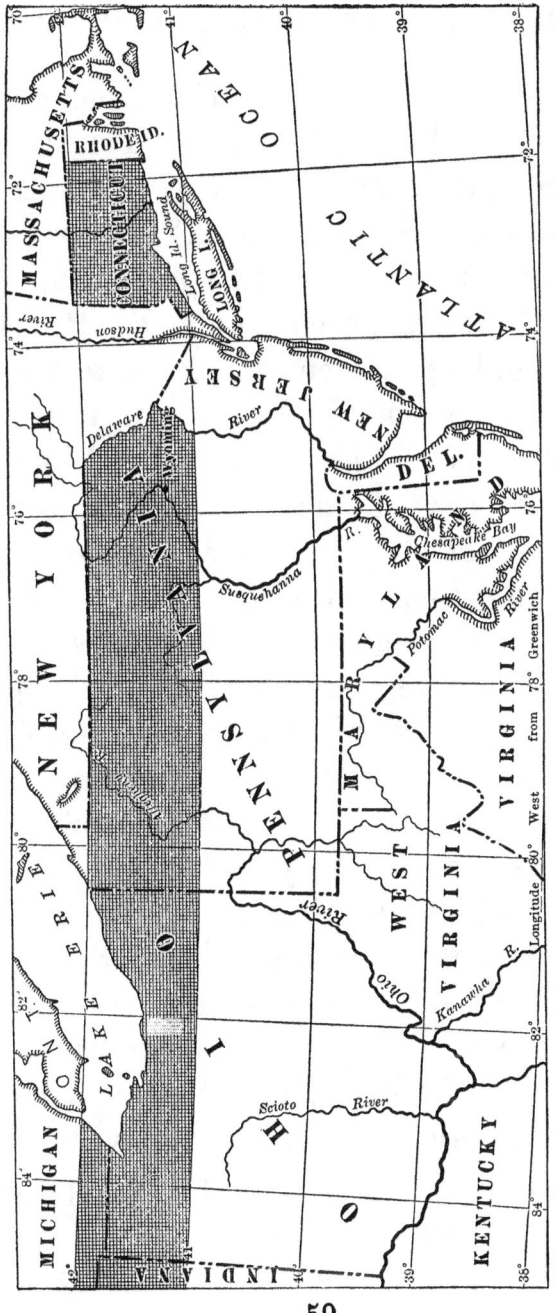

Map showing (by shading) parts of Middle States involved in the claim of Connecticut to lands extending indefinitely westward between the projected north and south bounds of her original charter.

Ohio and Her Western Reserve

it, to the extent of its breadth, from sea to sea, or "to the South Sea." This would have brought Connecticut's western extension nearly or quite down to the 41° of north latitude—almost to the Delaware Water Gap, and thus (had the claim been maintained) Pennsylvania would have been diminished to the extent of over two-fifths of its present territory.

Connecticut, in her strenuous endeavor to realize her early dreams of territorial expansion, was obliged by certain conditions in her charter to pass over the lovely valley of the Hudson and other territory of New York, which must have caused her acquisitive people a sharp pang of regret; but, curiously enough, she did not let this interruption of her claim bar her from seizure of the lands still farther west. Many of her sons looked with an intense longing to Wyoming, and some may have seen with prophetic vision the rich reward that awaited the meek in the inheritance of that part of the earth in the future State of Ohio which ultimately became the "Connecticut Western Reserve." The promised land was not to be relinquished without a struggle.

Wyoming

Pennsylvania's claim to the lands lying about Wyoming, the subject of the Connecticut contention, was as sound and just as to any within her charter limits.

The charter granted to Pennsylvania, upon the north, territory extending through the 42° or to the beginning of the 43° north latitude, thus overlapping by 1° the grant made to Connecticut by the same sovereign nineteen years before. Sir William Jones, the attorney of the Crown, had reported that: "The tract of land desired by Mr. Penn seems to be undisposed of by his Majesty, except the imaginary lines of New England patents, which are bounded westwardly by the main ocean, should give them a real, though impracticable, right to all of those vast territories." Thus the seed of strife was sown far away across the ocean; and fate so generously nourished the troublesome transplanted nettle here, that the Quaker husbandman labored in vain for half a century to clear it from the soil.

The peace-loving Quaker colony had been assaulted on all sides. Maryland and Virginia had endeavored to despoil her on the south,

Ohio and Her Western Reserve

and New York, and even New Jersey, had successively sought to secure a fraction of her dominion. These efforts were all brief, bloodless, without result.

But now Connecticut began, with well-organized system, persistent purpose, and strong promise of permanent success, what with the other colonies had been mere casual and ephemeral aggressions. The little Yankee colony seemed possessed of an irrepressible expansive spirit, which made it impossible for her to rest content within her bounds. As early as 1653 she had made a bold bluster of armed attack upon the placid Dutch of Manhattan Island, and threatened to annex certain towns on Long Island. The same restless pioneering and colonizing spirit which eventually led the Connecticut men to Wyoming, and caused the settlement of western New York and northern Ohio, had been active, fully forty years before the coming of Penn, in planting settlements on the Delaware.

There was thus nothing particularly new in Connecticut's purpose regarding the invasion of Pennsylvania. It was merely a later

Wyoming

manifestation of an old-time tendency turned in a new direction, a trifle more carefully planned, and very much more pertinaciously prosecuted.

Spies were sent to spy out the land, and it is probable that in the summer of 1750 some of these for the first time looked down from its flanking mountain wall upon the fair virginal valley of Wyoming. Three years later the Susquehanna Company was formed, and under this organization (consisting of 840 persons, afterward augmented to 1,200) it was proposed to occupy the coveted ground. The company, as its first step to this end, sent agents to Albany in 1754, to purchase from the Indians of the Six Nations the land in the Wyoming Valley. The Pennsylvanians had been alert to the danger that was menacing the province, but their protests were unavailing against the Susquehanna Company's offer of £2,000 of New York money; and the Connecticut men went away triumphant in the possession of the Indian title to the land, which they regarded as completing the legal title of their colony. Governor Hamilton of Pennsylvania about this time

Ohio and Her Western Reserve

wrote to the Governor of Connecticut remonstrating against the proposed settlement at Wyoming. Governor Wolcott of Connecticut answered in a non-committal but persuasive way, and at the same time touched upon what was really the key-note of the "Pennamite War," although it has very generally been lost sight of, even by usually careful historians, in viewing the complicated contention which ensued. Ignoring any response to the request that he should restrain the "invaders," he urged that those who became settlers should be made "freeholders," artfully arguing upon the inestimable value of ready and resolute defense to be rendered by men whose vital interest was thus enlisted, in case of French aggression. They should have something "to fight for of their own."

Now the heirs of William Penn owned the lands of the province in fee simple, and their policy was to settle the best of them under leases. Thus one of the worst features of feudalism was planted upon the soil of Pennsylvania. The question whether those who cultivated the acres they dwelt upon

Wyoming

should be serfs or freeholders really underlay the whole Wyoming controversy.

This explains, in a large measure, the sympathy which came to be extended to the Connecticut settlers by a considerable element among the Pennsylvania people. The "Yankee" settlers were of precisely the kind that the proprietors did not want, for they certainly were not of such character as to offer any promise of tractability or subservience to those ideas which governed the landed aristocracy. Herein lay the secret of the motive for the constant resort to official and military demonstrations by which the Penns sought the forcible expulsion of the settlers, rather than the employment of diplomacy to secure their recognition of the proprietary civil jurisdiction and the peaceful settlement of the northern boundary dispute.

Indian war intervening, the Susquehanna Company effected no settlement during all the years between its organization and 1762. But if idle, so far as outward appearances went, it was storing strength, and in the meantime the Delaware Company, having come into existence and bought an Indian

Ohio and Her Western Reserve

title, had settled Cushutunk, as we have seen, in 1757.

This first act of aggression aroused the Penns to a conviction that there would ensue a veritable invasion, and they took steps to fortify their title. They obtained from Charles Pratt (afterward Lord Camden), the attorney of the Crown, an opinion adverse to Connecticut's claim; but the Yankees were even better grounded in the law, for they had, not from one only, but from four eminent London barristers opinions against Pennsylvania.

Measures of coercion were resorted to by the Penns against the little colony at Cushutunk, proclamations issued, sheriffs' officers sent there with warnings, and a series of actions followed which constituted a prelude to the long contention at Wyoming.

The Delaware Indians, whose home was in Pennsylvania, complicated affairs by contending that they had been victimized by their old-time enemy, the Six Nations, who had "sold their lands from under their feet"; that they themselves, the real owners, had sold none at all.

Wyoming

Such was the situation when in the early spring of 1762 about 200 Connecticut men made the first settlement, under the auspices of the Susquehanna Company (about a mile above the site of Wilkesbarre) in the Wyoming Valley. This term was then, as now, applied to a stretch of the Susquehanna bottoms about 21 miles long and averaging 3 miles in width, shut in by actual mountain walls 1,000 feet in height. Fertile and fair as heart could wish, abounding in the richest growth of all that was natural to the clime, watered by the broad river and by innumerable cascades that leaped down the verdure-clad hills, it must, in its primeval condition, have seemed to those pioneers a veritable garden of the gods.

Though the Delaware Indians demanded of the Governor of Pennsylvania their immediate expulsion from the new-found Eden, nothing was done, and tranquillity reigned in the lovely land for two seasons. But it was only such calm as lulls to a false sense of security.

A storm was portending. The Indians were sullen. Their great chief, Teedyuscung,

Ohio and Her Western Reserve

had been mysteriously burned to death in his cabin by some of his Indian enemies among the Six Nations, but Indian cunning threw suspicion upon the poor Yankees. The Delawares, brooding for months upon the murder, and obtaining no satisfactory answer to their repeated demands that the settlers should be driven out of the country, at last, on the night of October 15th, fell in fury—but silently, without a single warning whoop—on the little village, and murdered 20 of its people. The rest fled, some to the lower settlements in Pennsylvania, some to Connecticut. This was the first massacre of Wyoming, not indeed an incident of the "Pennamite War," but an example of Indian ferocity in the resentment of real or imagined wrong, and an experience sufficient to deter forever any less pertinacious people than the Connecticut settlers from returning to the scene of its occurrence.

It did indeed keep Wyoming a wilderness for half a dozen years. But in 1769 the natural charms of the region had so far overcome the horrors enacted there, that the Yankees were constrained to possess them-

Wyoming

selves again of the valley. In February came a body of 40 determined men, sent out by the Susquehanna Company to occupy the country and defend it at all hazards against the Pennsylvanians. They were to be reenforced by 200 more and they were given land and money liberally for their services. They were commanded by a native of Connecticut, a resolute soldier, a hero of the French and Indian wars, who had gained honors also at the taking of Havana in 1762 —Colonel Zebulon Butler. He and his men built "Forty Fort," so called from their number, a mere blockhouse, but destined to be famous—the site of which is still prominently identified.

In the meantime the Penns had induced the Indians to repudiate their sale to the Yankees, and, on the principle that possession is nine points of the law, had founded a settlement in Wyoming, under one Captain Amos Ogden, an Indian trader from New Jersey, whose armed band Butler was not a little surprised to find there ready for resistance.

And now commenced a hand-to-hand con-

Ohio and Her Western Reserve

test for the lovely, fatally alluring valley, and practically for all that part of Pennsylvania between the forty-first and forty-second parallels of latitude—one of the strangest struggles in the history of the country—a contest having many of the elements of an *opera-bouffe* war, but unfortunately, a plenitude of tragedy, too.

Ogden opened the war by the arrest of the Yankee leaders, whom he marched through the woods to Easton jail, 60 miles away. They were speedily released on bail furnished by their followers and by some Pennsylvania sympathizers. Then Ogden arrested the whole 40, and the little jail received a glut of prisoners that fairly strained its walls, but again all went free on bail and trooped triumphantly back to Wyoming. By the next summer the settlements contained over 300 men, while more were constantly coming. Some of the later arrivals erected Fort Durkee, named in honor of their captain. Again Ogden appeared on the scene, this time with 200 men, and after he had captured Durkee by strategy, and sent him in irons to Philadelphia, the rest surrendered, possibly awed

ARREST OF THE CONNECTICUT SETTLERS.

Wyoming

by the appearance of a little four-pounder cannon which the warlike Ogden had unlimbered before the fort. The poor settlers were peremptorily put on the road to Connecticut.

Ogden now went to Philadelphia to receive applause after this first act of the drama, but he had scarcely heard the first congratulations of the proprietaries when news came that the little garrison he had left to guard the valley had been as summarily ejected as were the Yankees a few days before. And the worst of it was that the aggressors were Pennsylvanians, of the class who sympathized with the Connecticut people. They were under Captain Lazarus Stewart, and had moved with a spirit stimulated by the presentation of a whole township of land from the Susquehanna Company.

In this entry upon the scene of Stewart and his men we have a suggestion of one secret of the long continuance of the Pennamite Wars. They were not the only Pennsylvanians who actively sympathized with and succored the Yankees; and there were still more who, while they had no particular

Ohio and Her Western Reserve

love for the intruders, had none whatever for the Penns. These conditions made it well-nigh impossible for the proprietaries to sweep back, and keep back, the rising tide of immigration. It was not the powerful province of Pennsylvania, but the mere private family of William Penn, impoverished and unpopular, which was opposing the invasion. Had it been a matter of colony against colony, Pennsylvania would doubtless have prevailed over the intruders in one grand decisive action, and so summarily have ended the strife.

But, as it was, there followed a tedious and trying succession of strategic movements, skirmishes, sieges, counter-sieges, sorties, sallies, captures, capitulations, and evictions of one party or the other, all without permanent result.

The first blood flowed soon after Stewart's appearance in the valley, when, he having restored Wyoming to the possession of the Yankees, they were in turn attacked by Ogden's posse and one of the Connecticut men was killed and several wounded. This gave to future clashings of the two parties

Wyoming

an increased ardor, and from thence onward there were many sanguinary conflicts in this miniature war. Once after Ogden had been long besieged, and had finally to surrender, there came a period of five months of peace. Colonel Butler returned, recruits came with a rush, and there were new life and activity in the valley. But Ogden was again sent by the alarmed Penns to break up the settlement. A battle ensued in September, 1770, and several of the Connecticut men were killed, many prisoners taken, and all who could do so made their way to their old New England homes. This was the fourth time that Connecticut in Pennsylvania had totally ceased to be.

But the Yankees, as promptly and cheerfully as if nothing had happened, came back in the spring with bluff Colonel Butler again at their head, and hostilities reopened in earnest, which involved enough of thrilling adventure to constitute a whole Odyssey of woodcraft war. Finally, after Ogden had been summarily defeated, with the loss of nine men, an interval of peace ensued which lasted four years.

Ohio and Her Western Reserve

Up to this time Connecticut as a colony had not, at least openly, taken any part in the Wyoming controversy; but now, when there was for the first time some reason to think that the Penns had succumbed to the inevitable, the colony sought to extend government over the territory so long fought for by its subject, the Susquehanna Company. Accordingly, in January, 1774, Wyoming, Pa., was included in a county of Connecticut, under the name of Westmoreland, and shortly afterward a "town" was established, practically coextensive with the former, and of the same name. The principal settlement was duly named Wilkesbarre, in honor of John Wilkes and Colonel Isaac Barre, champions of the colonies in the British Parliament. The "town-meeting" idea, of New England root, flourished from the first, and soon burst into full bloom. Elections were held, and representatives sent to the Connecticut legislature. The great county of Westmoreland extended from the river Delaware westward 15 miles beyond Wyoming, and in extent from north to south was the whole width of the charter bounds. It thus included Cushu-

Wyoming

tunk (as we have already seen, the first settlement of the Connecticut people) and other settlements on the Delaware.

All told, some 6,000 people had now come into Yankee Pennsylvania. Peace had prevailed longer than the Connecticut men had ever before experienced it. But the isolation of one of the new, outlying settlements tempted a revival of Pennsylvania authority; and the success which attended the expedition of one Plunkett in destroying it made him such a hero that he was given a far larger force with which to strike a supreme blow at the stronger settlements.

There were other and entirely new circumstances, however, which combined to produce this action. The fate of Wyoming was still, indeed, in some sense, involved in the affairs of the Pennamite Wars, but the little ripples on the local sea of trouble were fast being swallowed up in the great ground-swell of the Revolution. Wyoming had for a time enjoyed peace *because* of the Revolution; that is, because the Penns, aware of its approach, and long cognizant, too, of the fact that their *régime* was not to the liking of a

Ohio and Her Western Reserve

majority of the people, had desisted from demonstrations which would attract to them undesirable attention. But now the rumblings of the Revolution, which had given Wyoming peace, brought it a revival of the Pennamite War; that is, of the Pennamite War with all of the Penn animus plus that of entirely new interests. In explanation, it must be said that the Penns had begun in 1771 to sell lands in Wyoming which theretofore they would only rent. Many Pennsylvanians had purchased, and so had strong personal motive for the expulsion of the Yankee settlers under Connecticut's claim.

And now came the year 1775 and the battles of Lexington and Concord. The war was begun. If it should end favorably to the colonies, there would attach to Wyoming a new and far greater value than that it had possessed under a feudal proprietorship. Therefore, many more Pennsylvanians became interested, and where it had formerly been a slow and difficult task to raise 100 or so men for one of the Ogden expeditions, 700 were quickly enlisted for Plunkett's. Men who until then had been entirely indifferent to

Wyoming

the welfare of Wyoming—such prominent Pennsylvanians as Morris, Meredith, Biddle, Shippen, Tilghman—were liberal contributors to the fund raised for the equipment of the expedition.

An army of 700 men, led by as plucky a commander as Plunkett, would at any time prior to this period have routed the Yankees from Wyoming, and a permanent garrison of half that number would have kept them forever from returning, but now it was too late.

Plunkett marched bravely up with his 700, a formidable train, and a field-piece or so; but Butler, with only half as many fighting men, beat him off in a decisive battle, and the Pennsylvanians hopelessly retired. Thus, by force of arms and with the blood of her sons, Connecticut had sealed the claim she believed just to the soil of a sister colony, and the Wyoming men now settled down to enjoy the loveliness of that land they had conquered and clothed with law. But their roseate hopes were doomed to a deep and speedy disappointment.

CHAPTER III

BATTLE AND MASSACRE OF WYOMING

NOTWITHSTANDING the fact that the Revolutionary War was in progress, and that many of the leaders and able-bodied men were withdrawn from the settlement, having patriotically entered the Continental army, Wyoming was blessed with peace and prosperity. Its people realized pretty closely the condition of those in the fanciful "Happy Valley" of Rasselas. So they might have continued to do, as far as any molestation from their old enemy, the Pennamites, was concerned; but a new terror was taking form. A great storm was gathering in the North, which was soon to shut the sunshine from the basking valley, and bring down in its place such darkness and devastation as, with all its tribulations, it never yet had known.

The powerful Iroquois, or Six Nations,

Battle and Massacre of Wyoming

with other Indians, allies of the British, had, until the defeat of Burgoyne at Saratoga, been held in the northern region; but now they were released, and their war-roused passion was to be wreaked on the defenceless border settlements.

The full fury of the savages was seemingly reserved for fated Wyoming.

There was a partial reason for this in one of the facts which linked with the Wyoming massacre, as an event of the Revolution, the miniature Pennamite War. The intense patriots in the limits of the Connecticut claim had, in 1775, aroused a general enmity among the Tories by expelling from Wyoming some forty of their number (mostly Dutch and Scotch-Irish of the Mohawk region); and of course they had incurred the most active and implacable animosity of the individuals whom they had cast out. These now added the venom of their vindictiveness to the composite malevolence brewing as in a caldron. They were associated with the Indians in all of their maraudings on the border; one of their number actually built a blockhouse in the upper part of Wyoming Valley to assist in masking the incursion, and it has been thought by many that their machinations were the chief influence in drawing the Indians thither.

As to the Indians who were regularly in the employ of the British, it is a curious fact that they had been long dominated—speaking in a broad way—by Sir William Johnson, and he in turn had been influenced to a considerable extent by one of their number—his mistress, Molly Brant, whose brother, Joseph, was the great captain of the Six Nations. But Sir William was now dead, and whatever of his old-time influence was continued came into operation through his son and nephew and Molly Brant.

As the signs of danger increased at Wyoming in the early summer of 1778, wives besought their husbands to return from the army, and the people generally clamored for protection, calling alike upon the Continental Congress and the Pennsylvania authorities; but no effective measures were taken by either for their aid. Finally, a number of the officers sent in their resignations, and a score or so of the privates deserting, they

Battle and Massacre of Wyoming

hurried to the threatened settlements. Among them was Colonel Zebulon Butler, who by common consent became commander. There was not only lack of men, but lack of ammunition; and as danger grew daily nearer, Colonel Butler, having already employed all of the males in scouting, strengthening the forts, and generally preparing for the threatened attack, now set the women all at work in a most strange undertaking—the actual manufacture of much-needed gunpowder, to which, even with the crude conveniences at hand, Yankee ingenuity proved equal. And while they leached saltpeter from the soil in the blockhouses, prepared charcoal, bruised quantities of each with pestle and mortar, blended them, cast bullets and rifle-balls— while the situation daily and hourly grew more tense, and no tidings of relief came— the enemy was rapidly massing in the North for an attack which the Wyoming people knew was inevitable.

The Indian and British and Tory forces were concentrated at Tioga toward the close of June, 1778, while its leaders sent a delegation of Seneca chiefs to Philadelphia to

Ohio and Her Western Reserve

put Congress off its guard, and at the same time sent spies down to Wyoming to ascertain, under the guise of friendship, the exact situation there and to disarm suspicion. But one of them (who was purposely made drunk) revealed enough to confirm positively the worst fears of the settlers—though even the holders of the extremest of these were far from foreseeing the sweeping, all-surpassing horror that was swiftly to fall.

And now, while this army—so soon to bring to Wyoming its crowning calamity and to engage in a sweeping butchery that was to appal the whole world—lies idle at Tioga, let us look at its composition and commanders. Surely no more heterogeneous herd of murderous soldiers and savages ever assembled in America. It has three elements, and in each many varieties. Its total is not far from 1,200 fighting men. First, there are 400 British provincials, consisting of Colonel John Butler's Rangers and Sir John Johnson's Royal Greens, with a rabble of Tories from New York, New Jersey, and Pennsylvania. Then there are not far from 700 Indians, chiefly Senecas, with detachments from the Mohawks

Battle and Massacre of Wyoming

and other tribes. The enemy is in almost every conceivable dress, and in appearance of every varying degree, from the martial dignity of the trained soldiers down to the ruffian type of the most abandoned and depraved of the Tories. The regulars are in smart uniforms—Butler's Rangers in rich green; the Tories and renegades in every form of backwoods rusticity and tattered motley; the Indians half naked or in savage attire, with their war-paint and barbarous adornment, varied with the martial trappings of soldiers slain in northern battles. With them swarms a band of squaws, if possible more bloodthirsty than their masters. Three classes, indeed; but well-nigh 1,000 diverse, fantastic figures, all actuated, however, by a single animus—a ferocious appetite for blood and the possibilities of paltry loot in the humble cabins of the doomed frontiersmen.

But if the rank and file and rabble of this nondescript assemblage are unparalleled in the border war of the Revolution for its complexity, the personalities of its commanders offer contrasts as strange and startling and incongruous. The expedition is avow-

Ohio and Her Western Reserve

edly under command of Colonel John Butler (a remote connection of Colonel Zebulon Butler, in command at Wyoming). He certainly led the British troops, and probably the Indians, at the actual time of the battle

and massacre; but the great Mohawk chieftain, Joseph Brant, now in his prime— aged thirty-six — the dignified and able semicivilized brother of Sir William Johnson's mistress, and the virtual head of the Six Nations, was with the force at Tioga Point shortly before it reached Wyoming, and, while he did not descend the river from that place and go into the fight, at least had some hand in assembling the Indians for the expedition. He had attained considerable education, and had translated the Bible into the Mohawk tongue.

84

Battle and Massacre of Wyoming

Colonel John Butler, commonly called at this time "Indian" Butler, offers a curious contrast to Brant, and is one of the most singular of the sanguinary characters engaged in the great strife. In Brant we see a superb, semi-tamed Indian, for the most part now reverted to savagery, but in whose naturally superior soul some sparks of humanity, engendered by contact with civilization, still glimmer. On the other hand, in Butler there is exhibited, in all that extreme reversion of the type of which the human is capable, the brutalized white man. He was a representative of a more than usually cultivated and gentle line, who had perversely sought savagery, and become more savage than the Indian himself; and now he was called "Indian" Butler, partly to distinguish him from his kinsman, Colonel Zebulon Butler, and partly for the simple reason that the *sobriquet* seemed supremely fit. "Indian" Butler was a descendant from a no less personage than that James Butler who was the great Duke of Ormond (1610–'88), of the ancient Anglo-Irish family which traced its genealogy to the dukes of Normandy before the Conquest.

Ohio and Her Western Reserve

He was, perhaps, the ablest, certainly the most atrocious, Tory leader of the period, and had figured as the commander of a motley band of marauding whites and Indians in 1776; had fought at their head in the battle of Oriskany, and had otherwise sought fame, and gained infamy.

Fat, and squat of figure, with round, rough visage, he was not in appearance an ideal leader, nor a man of prepossessing person; yet he was noted for his success in the former capacity, and he was not without agreeable traits as a heritage from his high ancestry, that not even his long life among scenes of blood, and his abandonment to more than savage cruelty, could wholly obliterate or conceal. In preparation for the proposed onslaught at Wyoming he was exceedingly active, and no detail escaped him. He was seemingly everywhere at once, never still, nervously but effectively bustling among soldiers, guerrillas, and savages alike, inciting them afresh from hour to hour, yet ceaselessly cautioning and exercising control.

If there was contrast between the dignified savage Brant and the excitable, degen-

Battle and Massacre of Wyoming

erate scion of nobility, "Indian" Butler, the final element of the incongruous and grotesque was reached in a third person of sinister and subtle influence in this strangely mixed mass of harsh humanity. This was a woman, no less than the redoubtable, eccentric enthusiast, "Queen Esther." Catharine Montour was the real name of this picturesque and gruesome figure in the strangest scene of the drama of the Revolution. She was a halfbreed, and the reputed daughter of one of the French governors of Canada. She had been liberally educated — possessed refinement, indeed—and the best society of colonial Philadelphia, of Albany, and New York had petted and fêted her as a romantic and engaging young woman, in whose veins coursed a mingling of cultured and savage blood. Soft hands had caressed her, and she was keenly sensible to the gentility of her frequent surroundings, and, in a sense, fitted for them; yet such are the contradictions of wild nature, however restrained temporarily, that this dusky, one-time favorite of stately drawing-rooms was the Hecate of the most horrible occurrence in the entire annals of savage war in America.

Ohio and Her Western Reserve

Queen Esther was a widow now—the widow of a chief—enjoying the repute of a seeress. At all times the possessor of a strange power over the people of her race, but now inflamed by the losses of her kindred, and very recently of a son, she had become a veritable fury, who swayed her followers into the utmost extravagances of fanaticism. Even the bloodthirsty Butler, the scourge of the border patriots, though he probably would hesitate at nothing in the way of rapine and murder, feared, upon politic grounds, the supreme ascendency of this fiery, insanely vengeful "Queen," and hence his activity among his troops, Tory rangers, and their red allies. That he did not wholly succeed was shown by the fact that when the final advance was made, Queen Esther became the actual leader of the Indian contingent of the army.

The wild aggregation led by "Indian" Butler and Queen Esther, 1,200 men—soldiers, Indians, renegade whites, all brutalized by three years of fierce frontier warfare; a majority by lifelong savagery; many incited

"Queen Esther" (Catharine Montour) inciting the Indians to attack Wyoming.

Brant and Indian Butler in background.

Battle and Massacre of Wyoming

by bitter personal animosity, and some by simple thirst for blood; energized by cupidity and cruelty; goaded by race hatred and by human hatred; urged on by all the craft of "Indian" Butler and the crazed cries of the zealot queen—finally advanced as if animated by a single will upon doomed Wyoming. The Indians descended the Susquehanna, their flotilla of canoes, in long, sinuous lines, following the current to a point a score of miles above the settlement, where they took to the shore to continue their advance. To the solitary Wyoming scout, who from his lofty mountain station watched every movement of this approach of the enemy, it may easily have seemed that some serpent monster passed the great curves of the stream and drew its slow length over the hills and along the plains—a monster, mightier and more malignant than the fabled ones of the medieval forests—moving slowly and inexorably, upon its prey.

It was highly characteristic of the hardy frontiersmen at Wyoming, that though they were fully aware that they were to be attacked by superior numbers and had only

Ohio and Her Western Reserve

vague hope of the arrival of reenforcements, the idea of flight seems never to have occurred to them. Their forces numbered, all told, only about 300 men, and nearly all of these, according to the inscription on the monument erected in their honor, were "the undisciplined, the youthful, the aged." There were 230 "enrolled men"—many, in fact, minors—and the remaining seventy were all either boys or old men. They embraced six companies, and were mustered at Forty Fort, on the west side of the river, where the families of the settlers on the east side had taken refuge. Such was the situation on that memorable day, the 3d of July, 1778, when the British and Indians, having advanced deliberately down the valley, feeling sure that their victims could not escape them, were finally met in battle. They had destroyed everything in their way. Jenkins's Fort had capitulated, a score of murders had been perpetrated, and Wintermoot's (which, as was afterward learned, had been built to aid the incursions of the Tories) had at once opened its gates to the invading host.

The settlers, with a desperation of courage

Battle and Massacre of Wyoming

rarely equaled in the history of war, resolved to put suspense at an end, actually marched forth to meet the enemy that outnumbered them four to one. Some few had counseled delay, and Colonel Zebulon Butler was of that minority, but he acquiesced in the verdict of the majority and led them out, the little force of 300, in the middle of the afternoon, with drums beating, colors flying, and in true military array.

There were six companies, and the officers of the little force, under Butler, were Colonels John Durkee and Nathan Dennison, Lieutenant-Colonel George Dorrance, Major John Garrett, Captains Dethic Hewitt, Asaph Whittlesey, Lazarus Stewart, James Bidlack, Jr., Rezin Geer, and Aholiab Buck. There were other officers in the battle which ensued, but without definite commands, as Captains Samuel Ransom, Robert Durkee, and William McKarrican. They marched up the valley, with the river upon their right. On coming up with the enemy the column deployed to the left and formed in line of battle, with its right resting on the high bank of the river and its left extending across the

Ohio and Her Western Reserve

plain to a swamp. Colonel Butler, supported by Major John Garrett, commanded the right wing, and Colonel Dennison, supported by Lieutenant-Colonel Dorrance, commanded the left.

The enemy then advancing, the colonel gave the order to fire, and a volley rang out along the entire line with precision and some effect. The British flinched and actually fell back before the Yankee spartans, but it was only for a moment, and they pressed forward again. Then with quick alternations of the orders "Advance!"—"Fire!" the brave Butler performed the almost impossible feat of moving his thin line slowly forward against the overwhelming force that faced it. But this well-nigh incredible resoluteness was all in vain, for even as the line advanced the Indians slipped singly and by dozens into the brush of the swamp and flanked its left.

On the side of the invaders "Indian" Butler, his subordinate officers, the Seneca chiefs, and even Queen Esther in person directed the fight in different quarters. Butler, divested of his usual Indian finery, and with a flame-colored handkerchief bound round his

Battle and Massacre of Wyoming

head, darted among his men, shrieking in his high voice orders to rangers and red men alike, and wildly evinced his delight as he saw the certainty of success, while his round face, red with his frantic excitement and intense activity, shone with a devilish triumph. The Wyoming men's left became confused, though the old men and boys did not retreat, and the Indians, seizing the opportunity, rushed forward with their frightful whoops and tomahawked right and left those still left standing. Many had already fallen under the murderous fire of four times their number. Lieutenant-Colonel Dorrance and Major John Garrett were killed; every captain commanding a company and nearly every lieutenant was dead. The little band melted like wax before a fire. The Indians pressed the survivors toward the river, along the bank of which wives and mothers of the brave fighters had crowded in agonized watchfulness. Some swam over and escaped. Others were pursued and tomahawked in the water or shot from the shore. A few, promised quarter, returned, only to be treacherously struck down as they climbed the bank. Several

Ohio and Her Western Reserve

found concealment on Monocacy Island, and others sought it only to be discovered and cut to pieces in their hiding-places, or dragged forth to be tortured at the leisure of their captors. It was there that one Tory killed his own brother, and that several other almost unbelievable horrors attested the atrocious fury of the assailants of these poor patriot settlers.

Massacre began when battle left off. One hundred and sixty men had been killed, and 140 had escaped—some only to be subsequently captured. Crack marksmen among the Indians had brought down officers and conspicuous fighters by breaking their thigh-bones or otherwise incapacitating them, so that they could by no possibility escape, and thus were reserved for torture a hundred times worse than death. Captain Bidlack was thrown alive on blazing logs, pinned down with pitchforks that happened to be at hand, and so held in spite of his powerful paroxysms until death relieved him. William Mason, a boy captain of a boy company, was similarly slain.

A debauch of blood followed for the

Battle and Massacre of Wyoming

especial delectation of Queen Esther. That seemingly insane savage ordered a score of the prisoners brought before her for torture, and her followers, springing to obey, quickly assembled them around a great boulder, known to this day as "the bloody rock." They were bound and compelled to kneel about the rock, and then this fanatic fury, who had once graced drawing-rooms and been the admiration of gentle dames, seized a heavy tomahawk, and, raising a wild song, swept swiftly aroung the circle and dashed out the brains of sixteen victims, while the warriors, crowded close about the scene of butchery, leaping and yelling, expressed their fierce joy. Four escaped from sacrifice at the hands of the savage queen, but fell not far away, for they were pursued by a hundred fleet-footed Iroquois. After all was over, there were discovered near bloody rock nine more corpses, all mutilated and scalped.

When night came on, the still insatiate savages built fires, and stripping the remaining prisoners naked, drove them back and forth through the flames, finally thrusting them on the embers with their spears, when

Ohio and Her Western Reserve

they fell from exhaustion, until all were despatched.

Altogether, in the battle and after, nearly 300 men were killed. Of the wretched people remaining, there were made that day in the valley 150 widows and nearly 600 orphans.

But a flight had already been begun while the massacre was in progress; and on the next day—after the arrival of ineffectually small reenforcements, and the surrender of the detachments of militia at Pittston and Forty Fort, and when the entire valley had been given over to the pillage of the Indians (whom Butler afterward said he could not restrain)—all the survivors of the tragedy followed in the footsteps of those who had fled at first.

The Indians, dividing into small bands, passed up and down the valley, burning every building and slaughtering all the inhabitants they found—except some children whom they carried into captivity. Finally, they rendezvoused and withdrew to the northward in a swarming, savagely triumphant body, the squaws bringing up the rear on

Battle and Massacre of Wyoming

stolen horses, their bridle-reins hanging heavy with strings of sodden scalps. As often the ludicrous treads hard on the heels of tragedy, so here with garish ghastliness these furies appeared fantastically garbed in the raiment of the slain settlers' wives and daughters— which they had abandoned in taking flight— while household spoils, pans, pots, kettles, ladles, and the like, clattered on the flanks of their horses, and added to the discordant din amid which the wild horde departed.

Desolation reigned supreme throughout the valley. In all directions there were only the charred ruins of cabins and the unburied dead, lying stark under the serene sky and pitiless sun of that 4th of July, 1778, where had so lately been happy homes and thronging, varied, busy human life.

In the meantime the wild flight of the survivors, begun while the battle still raged, or at least before the massacre, streamed through the wilderness to the Delaware and Lehigh settlements — chiefly to the safety afforded by Fort Penn, built by Colonel Jacob Stroud, where Stroudsburg now stands, near the famous Water Gap. This place of

Ohio and Her Western Reserve

refuge was only 60 miles distant, but the way lay over mountains and through almost impenetrable swamps, in a region absolutely uninhabited—the wildest part of eighteenth-century Pennsylvania. Frantic with fright, exerting every faculty, impelled by the one intense impulse of eluding the savage, of escaping death or awful torture, and with the vivid scenes of the horror in the valley ever before them, these pitiable refugees—men, women, and children—fled onward into the blessed protection of the forest and the hiding of night. This forlorn flight led into and through the great "Dismal Swamp of the North," or, as it was then, and is sometimes to this day called, "the Shades of Death." This was, and is yet to-day, a swamp upon a mountain-top, the vast, wet, marshy plateau of the Pocono and Broad mountains, an area still unreclaimed, included now in three counties, and surrounding the head waters of the romantic Lehigh. Over the greater part of this singular, saturated table-land there was a dense growth of pines and a tangled, almost impenetrable undergrowth, the whole interspersed here and

Flight of the Connecticut settlers through "the Shades of Death."

Battle and Massacre of Wyoming

there with expanses of dark, murky water, often concealed by a lush growth of mosses or aquatic plants, and swarming with creeping things, even as the matted forest abounded with wild beasts. But the terrors of the "Shades of Death" were as nothing now to these poor fugitives. Women, more than men, made up the throng. In one band upon the old "Warrior's Path" there were nearly a hundred women and children, with but a solitary man to advise or aid them. All were without food, many scarcely clothed, but they pressed on, weak, trembling, and growing constantly worse from their unaccustomed labor through the thickets, mire, and ooze. The aged sank by the side of the rude trail. One by one the weakest gave out. Some wandered from the path and were lost, some fell from exhaustion, some from wounds incurred in the battle, but the majority maintained life in some miraculous way and pressed on. The only manna in that wilderness was the whortleberry, and this they plucked and eagerly devoured without pausing. Children were born and children died in

Ohio and Her Western Reserve

the fearful forced march. One babe that came into the world in this scene of terror and travail was carried alive to the settlements. At least one which died was left upon the ground, while the agonized mother went on. There was not time nor were there means to make even a shallow grave. One woman bore her dead babe in her arms for 20 miles rather than abandon its little body to the beasts. Finally, the refugees reached Fort Penn and the towns of the good Moravians, where, half-famished, they were given food, and those who needed it tender care, until they could go to their old homes or find new ones.

CHAPTER IV

FAR-REACHING RESULTS OF THE MASSACRE

It needed no exaggeration in the story of Wyoming to fire the hearts of the colonists with a new zeal against the enemy under whose auspices the appalling deed of that July day had been committed. But in the meantime Wyoming was silently working in the minds of men far away a vaster result.

The significance of events—the relation of cause and consequence—is seldom seen contemporaneously, and sometimes not fully recognized when time has finally unrolled the scroll on which it is written, so slow are men to read aright. But in this case it did not take long to reveal the fact that Wyoming had won the heart of the world for the struggling colonies of America, against whom the mother country had armed and arrayed savages who could perform such atrocities as were

Ohio and Her Western Reserve

now told. What was of vastly more practical importance, it became apparent that the massacre had struck confusion into the camp of the Tories in England, who had to endure the odium of employing the Indians in subduing the rebellion; and finally, when men had gone far enough from the event to see clearly its meaning, they read that what had seemed at first an unmitigated disaster was in reality a disguised victory, and that Wyoming must take rank with Lexington and Concord and Bunker Hill in effect upon the long fight for freedom. The victims who fell in the valley before British muskets in Indian hands, and those slain by the tomahawks of savages who were British allies and commanded by a British officer, deserve a prouder monument than the one erected to their memory on the battle-field. They were really the marked martyrs of the Revolution, and the blood of the martyrs was the seed of independence and of the republic. These men—"the undisciplined, the youthful, the aged"—who marched out to battle against great odds, with guns poorly loaded with powder and ball made by their besieged

Results of the Massacre

women, in the awful deaths they died, supplied a mass of telling ammunition of fact to Edmund Burke and the Earl of Chatham which they employed against the Tory ranks in Cabinet and Parliament until the party tottered.

Another and later effect of the massacre abroad, was that for the first time an American subject engaged the pen of a British poet, and Thomas Campbell's Gertrude of Wyoming confirmed the renown of its author. It was not published until 1809, but long before that time it was given to the coterie which assembled at Holland House, and the tragic event which inspired the production, having become universally familiar to the English, had carried with its horrors the fame of the region which was its theater. The Wyoming Valley was the Yosemite of those days, but with the added interests of tragedy and romance, of the pastoral, and all the charms of sylvan solitude, so that it is not strange it appealed to the poetic mind and became in the imagination of Coleridge and Southey, the Lloyds and Charles Lamb, the ideal planting-ground for that projected ex-

Ohio and Her Western Reserve

periment in communal life which they called Pantisocracy, and for a long time cherished. With all that was written of Wyoming it is curious that its charms were not overdrawn, but they were not; and when in later years Halleck and Drake and Bryant and scores of prose writers came to dwell upon the beauties of the spot, each in turn seems to have been surprised that more had not been said in song and story of the most romantic region in all known America.

The bodies of the murdered men of Wyoming remained where they had fallen, a prey for the wolves and for the elements, until October 22d, nearly four months, when a military guard repaired there, and collected and buried them in one huge grave.

The blood of the martyrs cried aloud for retribution, and slowly but surely preparations were making to shatter the whole system of the hostile Indian alliance in New York. The once struggling settlement of the Susquehanna Company, looking only to its own people and indirectly to Connecticut for sympathy and support, now that it was struck

PRESENT ASPECT OF THE WYOMING BATTLE-FIELD.

A portion of Abraham's Plains, Exeter Township, Wyoming Valley.

Results of the Massacre

from physical being, had suddenly become a subject for general consideration. Washington himself was at the head of the movement for avenging its great wrong, and General John Sullivan, one of the best soldiers and most picturesque personages of the Revolution, being selected to "chastise and humble" the Six Nations, most effectually performed that duty.

Almost any other people than the Connecticut Yankees would now have abandoned Wyoming for all time, but these pioneers seemed not only to have been filled with the spirit of New England enterprise, but to have developed extra determination through longtime opposition. Many of them returned to the valley even in the autumn of the year forever made memorable by the massacre. They built a little fort and took up again their old manner of life, which was one of calm, matter-of-fact defiance of danger and death. The Indians made a notable raid in November, but the majority of the settlers never appear to have been greatly disconcerted. The tide of immigration was renewed and bore in a great throng. With the rank and file came

Ohio and Her Western Reserve

new leaders, among them Colonel John Franklin, destined to be one of the conspicuous characters in the militant new Connecticut.

Pennsylvania, during the Revolution, had made no attempt to renew hostilities nor to repeal the invasion, for the colony had been urged by Congress to remain inactive until the greater struggle was over. But as the Revolution drew to a close she prepared to resist aggression. The lands now belonged to the State instead of a private family, and there was an access of general interest in their disposal. A greater change in the situation, however, lay in the fact that there was a new power to appeal to for settlement—the Congress of the Confederation. There was impatience to have the question of ownership decided, and only a fortnight after Cornwallis's surrender, on November 3, 1781, a petition was presented to Congress asking that the case be adjudicated by that body, under the clause of the Articles of Confederation relating to disputed boundaries. It was finally agreed that the subject of jurisdiction should be left to a board of commissioners to be selected by the delegates from the two colonies,

Results of the Massacre

and those agreed upon were William Whipple, of New Hampshire; Welcome Arnold, of Rhode Island; David Brearly and William Churchill Houston, of New Jersey; Cyrus Griffin, Joseph Jones, and Thomas Nelson, of Virginia. On November 12, 1782, the court opened at Trenton, N. J. Distinguished counsel, including on both sides men then or afterward famous for service as soldiers, statesmen, and legislators, appeared before the tribunal —Eliphalet Dyer, William Samuel Johnson, and Jesse Root for Connecticut; and William Bradford, Joseph Reed, James Wilson, and Jonathan D. Sargeant for Pennsylvania.

It is a remarkable fact that although this court held a session of forty-one judicial or working-days, heard voluminous arguments from the full array of able attorneys—of whom one spoke for four days—and delivered a momentous decision, scarcely any record exists of its deliberations, nor in the century since has it transpired just what were the arguments made nor on precisely what ground was the verdict rendered. The judges had announced in advance that they would not make public the reasons which guided them to their decision, and they kept their secret inviolable. The verdict was flatly for Pennsylvania. "We are unanimously of opinion that Connecticut has no right to the lands in controversy," declared the judges, and they added: "We are also unanimously of opinion that the jurisdiction and preemption of all territory lying within the charter of Pennsylvania, and now claimed by the State of Connecticut, do of right belong to the State of Pennsylvania."

While it is reasonable to suppose that all of the old contentions concerning the charter claims were most minutely gone over, it amounts almost to a certainty that the tedious and dangerous dispute was decided more on the matter of *intent* than on the literal rendering of the fundamental documents, and that expediency was paramount in the minds of the judges to all other considerations combined. On its face, taking everything as literal, Connecticut's "real, though impracticable claim" would doubtless, in the estimation of an unbiased judge, have appeared better than Pennsylvania's; and yet that Connecticut should have jurisdiction over the great slice

Results of the Massacre

of Penn's province lying westward of her border, and so continuing westward "to the South Sea," would have been not only monstrously absurd, but dangerous to the public interest.

A new nation was entering upon the critical period of its formation, and its young life was imperiled by the conflicting claims of the very States that went to compose it. Massachusetts had a claim for millions of acres in western New York, on the same ground that Connecticut claimed a portion of Pennsylvania. Virginia and other States had similar imaginary mortgages on the West. Contention and bloodshed had already ensued, and the future threatened worse results than the past had developed. Somewhere a sacrifice must be made—a sacrifice of individual interests, or even rights—for the common good. The case in hand was that of Connecticut against Pennsylvania. Why not begin here? Such, in brief, it seems sure was the most weighty argument in the minds of the judges, and dictated the Trenton Decree. The opinion of public men, in surprisingly unanimous approval of the verdict, was strong testimony

Ohio and Her Western Reserve

to its wisdom and practical justice. It was a first, firm, forward step in nationality.

Another curious question that arises from the finding of the Trenton Court is: Did not the judges enter into a tacit and secret understanding with the Continental Congress that, in recompense for being deprived of her claim in an existent sister State, Connecticut should be allowed a grant from the lands farther west, which would inflict loss upon no single colony, because they were the common heritage of the new nation as a whole? Again there is not an iota of legal evidence on which to reply, but an affirmative answer is, nevertheless, almost compelled by the conditions which existed. Such supposition is rational, leaves nothing to be accounted for, satisfies one's sense of justice toward a long-suffering people, and is given strong support of a negative nature in the partial secrecy of the proceedings of Congress relating to the preliminaries of the grant to Connecticut of the Western Reserve, in Ohio.

The Wyoming men acquiesced quietly in the decree, but a new trouble arose. Jurisdiction had been securely vested in Pennsyl-

Results of the Massacre

vania, but the question of private ownership had not been touched upon, and therein lay the seed of a new contention which brought on a third "Pennamite War"—for, though the Penns were eliminated from the equation, the old name was retained. Pennsylvania, however near the right formerly, was now clearly in the wrong. Her people would not even allow the question of private ownership to be settled by a tribunal provided for in the Articles of Confederation. Thomas Jefferson sought in Congress to have such a solution of the problem resorted to, but a spirited remonstrance from the Pennsylvania Assembly put an end to the proceedings. In lieu of Jefferson's wise measure, the Pennsylvanians proposed an immediate relinquishment of half the Yankees' possessions, and an early relinquishment of all (with a slight time indulgence for the benefit of "the widows of those who had fallen by the savages"). These terms they resolved to enforce, and when the Yankees rejected the offer the matter was put for execution into the hands of that same Captain Alexander Patterson who had been conspicuous in the former contentions, and with two

Ohio and Her Western Reserve

companies of militia he repaired to the long-troubled valley. His first act was the summary arrest of Colonel Zebulon Butler, the old hero of Wyoming, and Colonel John Franklin. A flood assisted the designs of the Pennsylvania claimants and land jobbers. It swept away many buildings and obliterated some landmarks. Patterson's men did the rest. They proceeded to lay out the lands in accordance with the Pennsylvania survey, created new civil divisions, and even replaced the cherished name of Wilkesbarre with that of Londonderry.

In the middle of May the work of wiping Wyoming from the map was ruthlessly completed. The scenes that followed the massacre were now reenacted. The soldiery marched out and at the point of the bayonet dispersed at least 150 families, in many instances setting fire to their dwellings. Five hundred of the evicted—men, women, and children, infants in arms and old men—were literally driven from the valley, mostly on foot, poorly provided with food. They tramped through the mountainous wilderness toward the Delaware, only less miserable than the

Results of the Massacre

thronging refugees from the scene of the massacre six years before. Some died in the forest. Others reached the settlements only to succumb there to the rigors of their seven days' forced march—semi-starvation, exposure, and exhaustion. This was the seventh time the Connecticut people had made an enforced exodus from the valley.

The Pennsylvanians were in possession, but their high-handed method of procedure had alienated the sympathy of the right-minded of their own State. Shame and indignation led to the sending of a sheriff's posse to restore order, and the hasty recall of the evicted settlers. Patterson remained sufficiently in power to extend to the first who returned a warm reception, but finally, as the refugees rallied in greater force, Colonel John Franklin took command of them, and they went through the valley like a scourge, dispossessing the Pennsylvanians wherever they came upon them. Patterson, gathering his followers in a fort, stood at bay. A battle ensued in which men were killed on both sides. And so civil war again crimsoned the country. To quell this, Colonel John Arm-

Ohio and Her Western Reserve

strong—the same who was the author of the celebrated "Newburg Addresses" which had brought Washington's army to the verge of mutiny in the Revolution—was ordered with 400 militia to the scene of disturbance. It was the expectation that he would act impartially as a peace officer, but, like his colleague, Patterson, he hated the Yankees, and it was these only that he disarmed; and having done so, immediately declared them prisoners, manacled them in couples, and marched them to prison.

It is probable that now, but for the intervention of a peculiar Pennsylvania institution, the Council of Censors, and John Dickinson, who together created a new system for the Yankee settlers and mitigated the rigors of their prosecution, the colony of Wyoming would once more have been stricken from existence. But most of Armstrong's prisoners escaping, or being released, they swarmed back to the valley with that indomitable persistency they had exhibited for a quarter of a century, and resumed the defense of their homes. The conflict was now carried on in a desultory but determined way for years,

Results of the Massacre

and many lives were lost, both through the predatory Indian methods of war, involving the scouting of sharpshooters, and in collisions of considerable forces, before the war closed.

But cessation of armed hostilities in this case did not mean any improvement in the situation. Every change in the Pennamite Wars seems to have been to something worse. And now, while there was a respite from fighting, it was only because of the withdrawal of Armstrong and Patterson's soldiery; and the Connecticut men, who had so long battled for homes in Pennsylvania with numbers augmented by fresh arrivals and emboldened by partial success, were preparing for a *coup* which, had it been carried out, would have convulsed the country, and made its history read very differently from that we now have.

Civil war at the beginning, instead of seventy-odd years afterward, would very probably have rent the Confederation and possibly have precluded the formation of the republic itself; but civil war—and of very formidable dimensions, and over an issue well calculated

Ohio and Her Western Reserve

to shatter faith in the success of a democratic government—was precisely what the Connecticut people now meant.

The formation of a new State—it might have been the State of Franklin or Susquehanna—was not only contemplated, but actually commenced, and that it would have been consummated had not Pennsylvania finally accorded tardy justice is beyond doubt. Considering their experience with Pennsylvania and their long siege of complicated troubles, it is not strange that the Connecticut settlers at last conceived the idea of severing themselves from connection with the Quakers, and founding a new and independent State of which Wyoming should be the nucleus, and which they would probably have so carved as to contain all of Pennsylvania originally claimed by Connecticut; that is, all north of the forty-first parallel of latitude. By 1787 the new-State idea amounted to a furore in Wyoming, and there was an enthusiastic backing for the project in New England and New York. The plan was immediately upon its declaration to rush in a great mass of immigrants, to each of whom should be granted 200 acres of land,

Results of the Massacre

and maintain its existence and integrity against all assaults.

Colonel Ethan Allen, with the fresh prestige of leading the "Green Mountain Boys" to success, came out to Wyoming in the summer, and it has always been supposed was not only there to lend enthusiasm to the undertaking, but with a view to conducting a campaign of arms when the action of the long-oppressed settlers should precipitate attack. It is significant that he had been presented with several thousand acres of land by the Susquehanna Company.

Another remarkable man of the times, Colonel Timothy Pickering, also appeared, but he came as one of the Pennsylvania commissioners, and it was largely owing to his

Ohio and Her Western Reserve

skilful and astute handling of affairs that the most serious situation that ever confronted tortured Wyoming, and in fact equally threatened Pennsylvania and the country at large, was eased by diplomacy combined with judiciously decisive acts. He showed here much of that ability which enabled him in later years to adorn successively the high offices of Postmaster-General, Secretary of War, and Secretary of State, and to render acceptable service as Member of Congress and Senator of the United States from Massachusetts. He was originally from that State (to which he returned), and was chosen for that reason by the Pennsylvania Government, for it was believed that a New Englander could more effectively labor with the Connecticut men than could a Pennsylvanian. Pickering went among the Wyoming folk intent on making an equitable settlement of the vexed question and authorized to promise, in the name of the Government, that their lands should be confirmed to the settlers in clear title. Pennsylvania came reluctantly but of necessity to this concession, for her leading men had grown to fear that the unjust course which had been

Results of the Massacre

persisted in would bear bitter fruit. So it was with a mingling of the patriotic and politic in motive that the shrewd Pickering went on his mission. He took up lands under Connecticut title, cultivated the people, talked conciliation and concession, and almost at the outstart made an adherent of brave old Zebulon Butler. Simultaneously with Pickering's progress, very important work of a diverse nature went on in the States of Pennsylvania and Connecticut. The former passed what became famous as "the Confirming Act of 1787," expressly to disrupt the new-State movement; and at the very time, though the Quakers did not know how far it had gone, the Connecticut schemers were actually drawing up a plan of government for the proposed new State. Oliver Wolcott, of Connecticut, had written its constitution, while Major William Judd, of the same

Ohio and Her Western Reserve

State, had been decided upon for the first governor and Colonel John Franklin for lieutenant-governor.

Thus close had the new State come to bursting into being, when the legislative act of Pennsylvania and the diplomacy of Pickering averted the danger. But the colonel, redoubtable in peace as he had been in war, was still unable to swerve all of the Wyoming men to acceptance of his proposition. Not being able to conciliate his old companion in arms, Colonel Franklin, he forcibly captured him, put him in irons very promptly, and sternly hustled him off to Philadelphia, where he was clapped into prison and long languished under the charge of treason. As a sequel to this, Colonel Pickering was in June, 1788, arrested in retaliation, held as a hostage, and hurried from place to place by his Yankee captors, who for weeks eluded four companies of militia, a troop of horse, and a sheriff's posse.

Long before this the Connecticut settlers held a typical New England "town meeting" to discuss the question of accepting or rejecting the Compromise Act of 1787, which re-

Results of the Massacre

vealed the fact that a majority of them were in favor of accepting Pennsylvania's terms. Those opposed argued that the act confirming their titles had only been passed to stop the new-State movement, and time proved they were right, for in 1790 the Legislature repealed it as being unconstitutional. But the land-jobbing projects of the holders of Pennsylvania titles, who had brought about the repeal, gained nothing by the measure. There was in the act so much of wisdom and good policy, so much of justice to the long-suffering Connecticut men who had bought in good faith those Wyoming lands and expended their blood in defending them, that the spirit of the law actually survived and was potently active, even when the body of the act was dead and destroyed—stricken from the statutes. The settlers continued to hold their lands and were not again molested, though the legal war continued for years. The "Yankees" eventually made the State a trifling payment for the lands, and finally the last vestige of injustice toward them was wiped out by an act passed in 1807, exactly half a century from the date when Connecti-

Ohio and Her Western Reserve

cut's pioneers came to Cushutunk on the Delaware, and almost as long since the initial settlement at Wyoming.

What, now, were the ultimate results to Pennsylvania and rewards to Connecticut flowing from this unique invasion and unparalleled contention?

In a certain sense Pennsylvania was the chief gainer. Already having a more heterogeneous population than any State in the Union, she received still another distinct element, and the Yankee people who came among the Germans and Scotch-Irish either with or as a result of the Connecticut invasion—not, however, all locating at Wyoming—were by no means the least useful and influential citizens of the so-called Quaker State, as becomes evident on reflection that among the representative men of this blood were such statesmen as David Wilmot, of "Proviso" fame (who, in 1846, became a conspicuous figure in the great congressional campaign against slavery, in which, as we shall see, his Ohio compatriots of Connecticut origin were already engaged); Hon. Galusha A. Grow, Pennsylvania's veteran congressman-at-large,

Results of the Massacre

whose career covers half a century; Governors William F. Packer and Henry M. Hoyt; such able commanders of industry, colossal philanthropists, and college founders as Asa Packer and Ario Pardee, and such sterling city founders as the Scrantons.

Aside from the Connecticut contribution of men to Pennsylvania, thus merely indicated, perhaps the most important service that the Yankees rendered Pennsylvania lay in its initiative and example of the common-school system. They had been at Wyoming—as, indeed, wherever the New England colonies were planted—the pioneers of public schools and when Pennsylvania came tardily to establish these institutions she was influenced by the Connecticut element and found models on the Susquehanna which had existed for more than half a century.

With these facts in view, it is apparent that there were results of far-reaching good growing out of Connecticut's contest for Wyoming, which it is gratifying to chronicle; for without these there would appear a peculiarly pathetic and irreconcilable inadequacy of outcome for all those fifty years of stubborn strife.

Ohio and Her Western Reserve

As for the Yankee colonists, they secured clear title eventually to what is called "the seventeen townships" or about 300,000 acres of land, including the beautiful valley they had fought for for fifty years, from which they had seven times been evicted, and in which their people had twice been massacred. They had coveted and contested this ground for its agricultural worth and its picturesqueness; and curiously enough their heirs found the value of the lands doubled or deci-multiplied, and the loveliness of the land for the most part destroyed by one and the same cause—the discovery of anthracite coal therein, and the development of the most extensive mines in all America.

But the greater reward that came to the Connecticut people lay not in the country for which they had carried on their heroic, even if mistaken contest, but in the Western Reserve, which is a region a trifle larger than Connecticut, possessing a population almost equaling it at the last census, and exercising, in some respects, a power surpassing it.

In the granting to Connecticut of that huge tract—unquestionably influenced, as be-

THE WYOMING MONUMENT.

Erected in 1833, near the scene of battle and massacre of July 3, 1778.

Results of the Massacre

fore explained, by the idea that some measure of mercy, if not of justice, was due in compensation for its being deprived of possession in Pennsylvania—in its superb colonization and the consequences flowing therefrom—is to be found, historically speaking, the justification for the warfare at Wyoming.

The reward which Connecticut received in Ohio, for her otherwise well-nigh profitless persistency in Pennsylvania, was a reward of victory vicariously bestowed, inasmuch as it came, for the most part, to other men than those who had toiled in the Quaker State—and even to another generation—but it redounded hugely to the advantage of the State; and her people, as a whole, improved the opportunity newly opened to them to the very utmost.

New England well may boast
The band that on her coast,
    Long years ago,
Their Pilgrim anchor cast—
Their Pilgrim bark made fast—
Mid winter's howling blast
    And driven snow.
Long since hath passed away,
Each Pilgrim hoar and gray,
    Of that lone band ;
Yet where their ashes lie
Sprang seeds that shall not die,
While ever yon blue sky
    Shall arch our land !
Sons of that Pilgrim race
Were they from whom we trace
    Our Buckeye blood.
            LEWIS J. CIS

CHAPTER V

THE WESTERN RESERVE, OR CONNECTICUT TRIUMPHANT IN OHIO

CONNECTICUT heroically, even if mistakenly militant in Pennsylvania, where her sons had tried to carve a State from the territory which royal carelessness had bestowed both on William Penn and her own founders, became Connecticut completely triumphant in Ohio. A great host of her sons, undeterred by repeated disaster in warfare with the "Pennamites" for possession of the lovely valley of Wyoming, made an invasion of northeastern Ohio (while it was still a portion of the old Northwest Territory) every bit as peaceful and prosperous as that of the preceding generation had been troublesome and, so far as immediate result was concerned, almost profitless. They came in swarming thousands, absolutely unopposed save by the elements

Ohio and Her Western Reserve

and the wilderness, and theirs was here, in reality, the majestic march of a peaceful conquest most profound in consequence, because giving a mighty impulse to interior development. The contrast between the prompt and complete success of the Ohio settlement and the long baffled and only partial prosperity of the attempts at colonization in Pennsylvania was caused by the fact that in the later project Yankee shrewdness, profiting by early experience, had the way perfectly paved with law before her pioneers set foot in the coveted field. The Western Reserve, unlike Wyoming, was to them not merely a "promised land," but one actually conveyed by deed, signed, sealed, and delivered.

The settlement was hugely significant in several ways, but in none more so than in the fact that the pioneers of that vast army of occupation planted in the "New Connecticut," or Western Reserve, the last organized and distinct colony of Puritanism, which, as such, made a deep and historic impression upon the conscience of the country.

In the critical period of the old confederation preceding and preparing the way for

How the Connecticut pioneers came into the Western Reserve.

Connecticut Triumphant in Ohio

the formation of the United States, one of the most portentous problems that patriotic statesmen had to solve was the vestiture of all land claims in the General Government—the surrender of private pretensions for the public good. This problem—constituted by confusion in regard to the ownership of the Northwest Territory by the several colonies bordering it or lying easterly in the same latitude — darkened the prospects of the American Union, retarded the ratification of the articles of confederation, and threatened the very existence of the colonies. Thus menaced by grave dangers within, after successfully withstanding those from without, the country had arrived at a crucial stage when Congress appealed to the claiming States to make such sacrifices as should avoid discord and avert disaster. It was successful. New York responded first, and ceded her western claims to the United States in 1780. Virginia followed in 1784, but with a reservation, and Massachusetts in 1785; Connecticut coming last, reluctantly, tardily, and thriftily. Finally, by an act dated May 11, 1786, she relinquished "all her right, title,

Ohio and Her Western Reserve

interest, jurisdiction, and claim" to lands within her chartered limits "*lying west of a line 120 miles west of and parallel with the western boundary line of the State of Pennsylvania.*" But all within her chartered limits for 120 miles westward from Pennsylvania, and lying between latitudes 41° and 42° 2' north, she *reserved* from conveyance, and hence came in time the name "Western Reserve of Connecticut." Congress after a protracted debate accepted the cession on May 26th, and it was duly confirmed by deed on September 14th, following.

As the Yankee colony's charter claim extended "westward to the South Seas" (as is shown with other details in Chapter II), it was vast enough surely, but it was vague; and she therefore simply and shrewdly surrendered a huge, uncertain claim, impossible of support, attenuated almost to an abstraction, for something concrete, conveniently condensed, specific, positive, and practical. It was as if she had relinquished a few thousand miles of atmosphere, elusive, intangible, for sure title to a tract of solid ground with definite boundaries, as large as the mother

Connecticut Triumphant in Ohio

State (and at this day sustaining almost as great a population). This was certainly a bargain of the proverbial Yankee trader kind raised to its highest power.

Now, why, at a time when the public lands were regarded with an intense jealousy, was Connecticut thus gratuitously granted such a broad and bountiful domain? Her title, strictly interpreted, was clearly insufficient to secure her in possession. She had already been divested of it in Pennsylvania, where she had brought it to definite issue. But was not the blood of her martyrs, mistaken as they were, considered in the final account? And were there not questions of public policy involved which had weight in the consideration?

The acquiescence of Congress in the terms by which this vast and valuable tract of land was "reserved" by Connecticut only receives full explanation when we glance back to the decision of the Trenton court of 1782, and see that Connecticut was then divested of title and jurisdiction in Pennsylvania, notwithstanding her charter claims, long time possession, and the patient, persistent, blood-

Ohio and Her Western Reserve

expending bravery of the men of Wyoming. That the decision, both by intention and in effect, was for the general good is indisputable, but that the heroism and appalling losses of the Yankee invaders was entirely ignored is inconceivable. Thus the theory that, as an offset for the deprivation then necessarily inflicted upon her, and as a mark of recognition of her struggles at Wyoming, a secret compact was made with Congress that Connecticut should in the future receive a grant from the public domain, affords the only elucidation at once of that court's action and the surprising smallness of congressional opposition to the bestowal of what amounted virtually to a State upon the colony formerly dispossessed. That such an understanding was entered into is argued from the very absence of all record concerning the deliberations of the court and its reasons for the handing down of the decision; also by the paucity of report upon the proceedings of Congress in the matter of granting the desired lands to Connecticut.

In the absence of a solitary scrap of positive information upon the subject of a com-

Connecticut Triumphant in Ohio

pact, it is as probable as any surmise that can be made in history that the compact did exist, and that supposition almost, if not quite, universally entertained by students, not only explains all the existing circumstances, but accords to the court and the Congress of the Confederation that unfortunately rare blending of common sense with broad, untechnical justice and saving shrewdness which constitutes true statesmanship.

One strong piece of presumptive evidence that Connecticut's Pennsylvania experience figured as a factor in her favor when the granting of the Reserve was under consideration, lies in the fact that it was definitely stated that the boundaries had been so set as to make the grant equal to the amount of lands of which Connecticut had been divested in the Susquehanna country. Then, too, Pennsylvania voted from the first for the acceptance of the cession, which equally meant the allowance of the Reserve. There was some opposition, but all the States save Maryland came to the support of the measure, and it was passed in a fortnight from the time of its introduction. In addition to the

Ohio and Her Western Reserve

desire of Congress to render to Connecticut justice which was at once poetic and practical, that patriotic and businesslike body was keenly alive to the desirability of putting the public domain in the market for the purpose of revenue.

Washington was opposed to the allowance of the Reserve. So were the Virginians in Congress, though they ultimately voted for it. It was with something of ill grace that they sought to defeat the measure at any stage of the proceedings, for Virginia herself already had quite as large a reservation in Ohio as that sought by Connecticut. But, as will be duly shown, one great Virginian, John Marshall, afterward rendered important service to the people of Connecticut's Reserve, and so became connected with its history.

The reasons that finally swayed the Virginia Congressmen to approve the grant, says Mr. Grayson, one of the Old Dominion's delegation, writing to Washington, were "that the claim of a powerful State, although unsupported by right, was under the present circumstances a disagreeable thing; that sac-

Connecticut Triumphant in Ohio

rifices must be made for the public tranquillity as well as to secure an indisputable right to the residue" of lands; that Connecticut would settle her reservation "immediately with immigrants who would form a barrier not only against the British but the Indian tribes"; and that the settlement would "enhance the value of adjacent territory"—all of which was good logic and not very far amiss as prophecy.

The effect was, in general, such as was hoped and predicted. After necessary preliminaries, involving the perfection of Indian title and the adjustment of some of its domestic affairs by the company, a strong current of Connecticut immigration—long checked at Wyoming, but gathering strength as a stream does to surmount or evade a barrier thrust in its way—flowed onward like a great surging tide into the Ohio country. The grant to Connecticut helped to foster the sale to the New England Ohio Company, composed mostly of Massachusetts men, that organization which through its agent secured the passage of the "Ordinance of Freedom," laid the fundamental law upon the land, and planted

Ohio and Her Western Reserve

the first settlement northwest of the Ohio River.

The Indian tribes were threatening, and the same Brant whom the Yankees had sufficiently known at Wyoming—though he had no personal share in the work of massacre—the master mind of the whole red race at that time, as he had been in the border wars on the New York frontier, was at their head. But in the summer of 1795 General Anthony Wayne, having the year before most severely chastised the allied hostiles, concluded with them the treaty at Greenville which released, among others, the greater part of the lands in the Reserve—and, happily, was never violated. Thus the last vestige of impediment to immigration being removed, the Yankee State put its lands in the market. Indeed, she had anticipated the outcome, so that the extinguishment of Indian title and the sale of the lands were practically simultaneous.

Most important of the steps anticipatory of the sale was Connecticut's reservation from the sale of her own Reserve of half a million acres of land constituting the western end of the tract. This she had, in 1792, in response

Connecticut Triumphant in Ohio

to numerous urgent petitions, set apart for bestowal upon her citizens who had suffered by "incursions of the enemy during the late war," and the tract was therefore then called the "Sufferer Lands," but later (because most of the sufferers were losers by fire, in the Connecticut towns burned by the British) it was given the name it bears to this day—"the Fire Lands"—of which further mention will be made.

The resolution authorizing the sale of the Reserve—excepting the half million acres of Sufferers' Lands—passed the Legislature at a session held in Hartford in May, 1795, and shortly afterward the committee appointed for the negotiation effected a sale in separate contracts with forty-eight individuals, realizing for the State the sum of $1,200,000. The amounts paid varied from eight or ten up to $168,180, and each grantee became an owner of such a proportion of the entire purchase as the amount of his contract bore to the total sum. Thus Pierpont Edwards, who engaged to pay $60,000 toward the purchase, received a deed for sixty thousand twelve-hundred thousandths, or just one-twentieth of

Ohio and Her Western Reserve

the Reserve. The forty-eight purchasers, in the autumn of the same year, with a few others, formed the Connecticut Land Company, the membership of which was ultimately increased to several hundred.

Right here a mere glance at the names of the original purchasers and early members of the land company is alone sufficient to reveal the fact that the western movement of Connecticut, which realized its largest result in Ohio, was, from the start, one of high character and distinguished *personnel*, and that while it enlisted at the outset the interest of the leading capitalists of Connecticut, they were not merely men of financial force, but represented in various forms the very van of the varied active ability of the time. Several of them were already noted; others destined soon to become so. Moses Cleaveland was a patriot of the Revolution, and he became the founder of the chief city in the Reserve. The names of others, as Coit, Austin, Newbury, Ely, Kelly, were eventually written upon the geography of the Reserve to remain forever. Caleb Atwater was one of the leading scientific authorities of the time; Samuel Mather, who rep-

Connecticut Triumphant in Ohio

resented in the purchase a number of associates in Albany, N. Y., represented in heredity the clerical family of Cotton, Increase and Richard Mather—certainly an appropriate line for the perpetuation of Puritanism in the New Connecticut. Gideon Granger, who had $80,000 worth of stock in the great land purchase, was to fill the office of Postmaster-General for fourteen years, dating from 1801, and to gain a Junius-like reputation in political writing over the signature of "Algernon Sidney." Oliver Phelps, the nabob of the company, who was interested to the amount of over $200,000—$168,000 individually and the balance in a partnership subscription with Gideon Granger—was a great merchant, and heavily interested in New York lands, for the disposition of which he had opened at Canandaigua the first land office established in America. He was the leading land speculator of the time. Pierpont Edwards, though born in Massachusetts, was a son of that stanch Connecticut metaphysician and theologian Jonathan Edwards, was himself a patriot and an able lawyer, a member of the Congress of the Confederation, and as the founder of the "Tol-

Ohio and Her Western Reserve

eration Party" in Connecticut, which had made him extremely unpopular with the Calvinists, might be regarded as a kind of a personal forerunner of the larger liberality with which the original essence of Puritanism came to be diluted, and its asperities in some measure displaced by amenities in the New Connecticut. The descendants of Pierpont and of Jonathan Edwards were among the pioneers, and the family—with those of several other of these notable personages among the purchasers—is prominent in the New Connecticut to-day.

Such, in brief, were a few of the fathers of the westward expansion movement of Yankee spirit. They practically furthered by money and influence the settlement of the Reserve, while the State, with the $1,200,000 which they paid into her treasury, in those days when a million was yet a mighty sum, thriftily turned around and bestowed the bounty upon her schools. Not all of them were among the immigrants, but it is safe to say that the families of nearly all were represented, and the names of most of them figure in the annals of the Reserve and are prominent in the affairs of the present day.

Connecticut Triumphant in Ohio

The lands having been purchased, the next thing in order was their survey, and for the accomplishment of this the company sent out an expedition in May, 1796. It consisted of fifty men and two women—five surveyors, a physician, chainmen, axmen, hunters—all able-bodied, energetic, eager for the sight of the promised land, the fame of which had been already industriously spread through the mother State and New England.

The Moses who led these children of Connecticut through the wilderness was General Moses Cleaveland. In this sturdy commander of the half hundred surveyors we have the first actual pioneer—one of the most prominent characters of the colony and the founder of its future metropolis. It is notable, too, that like so many others who had a part in the beginnings of the New Connecticut, he was an officer of the Revolutionary army. He was a man of culture,

Ohio and Her Western Reserve

too, a graduate of Yale, a lawyer by profession. He was born in Canterbury, Windham County, in 1754, and died there in 1806.

The expedition was a formidable undertaking. The party rendezvoused at Schenectady, N. Y., whence they ascended the Mohawk in four flat-bottomed boats. Their way led by Oswego, Niagara, and Queenston to Buffalo. Besides the toilsomeness of the journey they encountered some opposition from the British at the frontier forts, who had not yet been officially apprised of the passage of Jay's treaty, which made the navigation of the lakes free to American vessels, and they had to resort to a little strategy to get by. Then at Buffalo, where the navigators to their satisfaction met the overland contingent of their force which had been entrusted with the bringing on of their horses and cattle, they also met Seneca and Mohawk Indians, with Brant and Red Jacket as their leaders, to whom they made presents. Then the fifty surveyors went on by way of Lake Erie, hugging the shore and admiring the bluff, forest-clad banks, until they reached the mouth of a little creek now known as Conneaut, and

Connecticut Triumphant in Ohio

here they landed first on the soil of the Reserve marking the Plymouth of the western Pilgrims.

This vanguard of the army of occupation made its arrival on July 4th, and from this circumstance they named the place Port Independence, and with the spirit of the day, heightened by their generally prosperous passage to the West and the golden prospect held before them by the new land, they proceeded to celebrate. They fired the national salute with half a dozen fowling-pieces, pledged each other in the sparkling liquid from the lake, called down blessings upon the land many of the little company had assisted in wresting from the British grasp, made glowing predictions of the future greatness of the new nation and the colony they were about to plant, and sat down with thankfulness to a bountiful dinner in which were many reminders of the old Connecticut, while their imaginings wandered forth to the new. It is doubtful, however, if any of them conceived possibilities approaching the actual realization that Time was holding in store for the region stretching as an absolutely virginal wilderness a hundred

Ohio and Her Western Reserve

and a score miles westward from their camping-place.

Among the toasts they drank were "The President of the United States," "The Connecticut Land Company," and "The State of New Connecticut," the last of which would indicate that the spirit of Yankee expansion did not stop short of State-making—an idea which had its inception during the troublous times of Wyoming. But scarcely had they finished feasting when the Indians came upon them again—not, indeed, with tomahawks as in the old days in Pennsylvania, but with questions and demands, as at Buffalo—asking why the white man encroached upon the red man's hunting-ground?—a question which was not answered, but peaceably parried with some beads and a keg of rum.

Cabins having been built for the surveyors, General Cleaveland left them to their work, and with a few of his staff coasted westward in an open boat along the south shore of Lake Erie, their objective point being the mouth of the Cuyahoga, which they duly reached, and were greatly gratified by the prospect afforded by the high ground, luxuriantly tim-

Connecticut Triumphant in Ohio

bered, which lay between the river and lake, on the eastern bank of the former, and fronted both with bold bluffs. The leader gave orders that this site, possessing almost all possible natural advantages, should be surveyed into city lots, which was speedily done, and the members of his party proposing that it should be named in honor of their commander, he accepted the compliment, and the city of Cleveland was thus founded.

The Moses of this march, if he smote no rock to bring forth water, yet performed an act there in the wilderness in that summer of 1796 the consequences of which have flowed on in an increasing tide of prosperity for more than a century, and in the present metropolis of the New Connecticut, with its 400,000 people, has more than realized the fondest hope of its founder—for his extremest prophecy was only that the town would ultimately equal Windham, Conn.

Colonel James Kingsbury, with his wife and three children, seeking a home in the West, had joined the surveying party at Buffalo, and theirs was the first family settled upon the site of Conneaut, and consequently the first

Ohio and Her Western Reserve

in the Reserve. Another child which came to this family was the first born of the new colony, and its little life succumbed to the rigors of the winter succeeding its birth. Thus in a single round of the calendar the cardinal events of human experience were enacted in the vast lonely wilderness, a few years hence to teem with busy life. The Kingsbury family's experience of one winter alone in the woods was such as to make them yearn for a little human companionship, and as they could expect this at the mouth of the Cuyahoga, they went on there, and in June, 1797, became the first permanent settlers of Cleveland.

The only predecessor of Kingsbury as an actual resident of the Reserve had been that eminent Revolutionary character General Samuel Holden Parsons, of Lyme, Conn., who as the grantee of the "Salt Spring Tract" of 25,000 acres had become, in 1788, the first individual land-owner, but he had lost his life in 1789 upon his property, in what is now Mahoning County.

Lorenzo Carter with his family became the first neighbors of the Kingburys, and the

Connecticut Triumphant in Ohio

total population of the settlement, comprised in two families, amounted to nine persons. A family named Stiles had wintered here, and General Edward Paine, who afterward located farther east, sojourned with them; but to all intents and purposes the Kingsburys and Carters were the pioneers, and became the first permanent residents of Cleveland and of the Reserve.

This same Carter was a character of marked interest in the little community. He may be considered as the founder of Cleveland's commerce, and as a born trader and the possessor of a peculiar backwoods diplomatic ability, he was invaluable in the management of the Indians who flocked about the settlement— a service in which great native shrewdness was supplemented by the almost invariable employment of whisky distilled upon the spot as early as 1798 by one of the pioneers.

He overshadowed the more highly educated and dignified Colonel Kingsbury, notwithstanding the fact that the latter, in 1800, was made the first Judge of the Court of Common Pleas and Quarter Sessions, and in local influence and usefulness even surpassed Samuel

Ohio and Her Western Reserve

Huntington, a learned lawyer of aristocratic bearing, the nephew, namesake, and *protégé* of that Governor of Connecticut who was a signer of the Declaration of Independence, and who himself became the second Governor of Ohio. But this gifted son of Connecticut, with his intense activity, his elegant manners, probably gained in France, the leading representative, in the region, of the dying but proud Federalist party, probably only prevented by his own untimely death from holding an even more exalted office than that of chief executive of the State, was for his time the dominant public character of the New Connecticut. He helped to give the State its earliest impetus of political prestige, though he could not stem the tide of the Jeffersonian Democracy which here as elsewhere ultimately swept all before it. In the War of 1812, when the fortune of American arms in

SAMUEL HUNTINGTON.

Connecticut Triumphant in Ohio

the West seemed irrevocably shattered, he accompanied Lewis Cass to Washington, and he was second only to him in securing funds for the relief of the dissatisfied soldiers and the restoration of military spirit and an invincible front in the whole lake region.

The settlements gradually extended. General Edward Paine, who had been a sojourner among the pioneers at the mouth of the Cuyahoga, soon selected a beautiful site thirty miles east of that locality, where John Walworth had already located. He founded the town of Painesville and a family prominent in the varied walks of life which gave to the Union army in the civil war two very able generals. Hither, too, came Samuel Huntington, whom we have seen at Cleveland, and here he ultimately made his home, and died in 1817.

Prior to this, probably in 1798, came the first pioneers to the township five miles west of Painesville, perhaps the highest type of the Ohio farming community, Mentor, destined to be made famous as the home of the first President whom the Reserve gave to the nation. About the same time John Young, the founder of Youngstown, located in the south-

Ohio and Her Western Reserve

eastern part of the Reserve, and tiny improvements—little openings in the dense forest where the sun was permitted to reach the rich soil shaded for centuries while it gathered strength for the husbandman—began to appear at long intervals in all directions.

An event of importance occurred on the 10th of July, 1800, when the region was given a government. The State of Ohio was still two or three years in the future, but it was characteristic of the Connecticut settlers that they should want and move actively for the establishment of law and order, and hence they secured the erection in one immense county of the whole Reserve, which is now divided into a dozen counties. This was Trumbull County, of the Northwest Territory, named in honor of Jonathan Trumbull, then Governor of Connecticut, and son of the original "Brother Jonathan." Its seat of justice, where court was held the same summer, and also the first election, was Warren, one of the half-dozen principal settlements, and, save Youngstown, the only one far inland.

This civil organization had only now become possible through the settlement of a

Connecticut Triumphant in Ohio

curious and troublesome tangle in the matter of jurisdiction over the lands of the Reserve between Connecticut and the United States. The solution of the difficulty (which was embarrassing the land company by clouding its titles and so retarding sales and settlement) devolved upon John Marshall, of Virginia, who, as chairman of a committee of Congress, exhaustively reviewed Connecticut's claims, and recommended the acceptance of her cession of jurisdiction by Congress, and the release to her by the United States of all right, title, and claim to the soil. This was duly accomplished by the passage of what was called the "Easement Act," and thus it was that John Marshall, of Virginia, who in a few months was made the first Chief Justice of the United States, became entitled to the gratitude of the Connecticut men for the institution of law in the Reserve and the removal of the last bar to its development. The stimulus of assured civil order and of cloudless titles gave a new and powerful impetus to immigration, and during the next decade the population of the Reserve bounded from 1,300 to a little over 16,000 souls.

Ohio and Her Western Reserve

In connection with this matter, other causes of growth may be briefly noted. Perry's victory off the shore of the Reserve brought a new attention to the region, and when the War of 1812 was ended immigration was renewed with a rush, and the epoch of true prosperity was begun in New Connecticut. It was a piece of wonderful poetic propriety and eloquence by which, a few years later, the same guns that had thundered aboard Perry's fleet were employed to proclaim the opening of the Erie Canal. Placed along its lines, about ten miles apart, their resounding boom, one after another in quick succession, carried the news from Buffalo to New York that an all-American waterway was open from Lake Erie to the sea. This was a consummation of consequence to the Reserve which had theretofore only an imperfect outlet for its surplus crops by way of Pittsburg. The completion

Connecticut Triumphant in Ohio

of the Erie Canal gave another powerful impetus to immigration, but, even better than that, it suggested the Ohio Canal, which eventually connected the lake with "La belle rivière," and even when completed, in the late twenties, as far as Akron, became not only of immense influence in the improvement of the country, but a potent stimulus to the commercial prosperity of its future metropolis, the city of Cleveland.

Returning now to the time of the pioneers, say to 1800, it must be noted that in some respects their experience was peculiar. It is rather to moral conditions than to backwoods adventure that one must look for the characteristics of early-day life in the Reserve. Only the very earliest of the settlers—the actual vanguard—encountered the perils, or even the worst hardships, that we are accustomed to associate with the pioneering life. There never existed here anything like that incessant, ever-lurking deadly danger from Indian hostility which those earlier Connecticut adventurers had experienced in Pennsylvania. There was, to be sure, an indefinite sense of danger, a vague apprehension, but it

Ohio and Her Western Reserve

soon wore away, for the few isolated cases of violence were only such as might occur from sporadic lawlessness in older communities, and the general impression which the Reserve received of the red man's character was a favorable one. Even the wild animals of the great unknown forest (though sometimes a cause of fear and trembling to the women and children in their lonely log cabins, especially when the prolonged and dismal howling of the wolves was to be heard at night) were regarded upon the whole as a providential blessing rather than an evil, for from the varieties most numerous the family larder was provided with much of its meat. Governor Huntington, it must be admitted, was attacked by wolves and well-nigh dragged from his horse (and, too, right where is now the most sophisticated and elegant part of famous Euclid Avenue); but such occurrences were rare, and the annals of the Reserve are rather painfully lacking in stirring story.

Pioneer life in this part of Ohio was peaceful, and almost from the first held out not only the promise but the substance of prosperity. Still, it contained those elements

Connecticut Triumphant in Ohio

of rude but idyllic rusticity, that romance of the remote and isolate, which came with long looking into the solemn solitudes of the vast forest, which all people of the olden time have endeavored, and usually in vain, to define.

CHAPTER VI

THE RESERVE A CONSERVATION OF CONNECTICUT

GRADUALLY the wilderness got the institutions of civilization. These were generally of the Connecticut brand, and bore its strong characteristics until modifying influences accomplished their work. Thus the early religion of the Reserve was Congregationalism slightly relaxed from the coldness and austerity of Connecticut's. Such bookish culture as there was—and it was far more conspicuous here than in most frontier communities—bore the odor of Yale. Up to 1800 the Reserve had neither church nor school, but it was very soon to possess both and in abundance. The pioneer preacher was the Rev. Joseph Badger, a native of Massachusetts, who was not located over any special flock, for the very good reason that when he arrived there were not enough people in any one settlement to form a church organization; but he belonged to the whole Re-

A Conservation of Connecticut

serve, and went about on horseback, visiting all in turn—a typically stalwart and zealous but more than usually learned backwoods missionary. He made his advent and began his large labors in 1800, and in 1801 we find him a pioneer of education as well as of religion.

It is a remarkable fact, and one illustrative of the distinguishing tendency of the Connecticut colony, that only five years after the first settlers entered the unbroken forest they should be seeking to plant there not merely a primitive district school, but an institution of advanced learning—an academy. It is more significant than any other isolated circumstance we can chronicle that, in 1801, when the population of the entire Reserve did not number over 1,500, a petition prepared by Minister Badger was presented to the Territorial Legislature praying for a college charter. It was not granted, but when the State had been organized and the first Legislature assembled, it passed an act incorporating, where but eight years before the Indians roamed without ever seeing a pale face, "The Erie Literary Society." The Rev. Joseph

Ohio and Her Western Reserve

Badger was one of the incorporators, and David Hudson was another, and the school they with their fellow pioneers established was the germ from which grew up at the town of Hudson, Western Reserve College—"the Yale of the West"—of which more anon. The Erie Literary Society established the first school of the kind in the New Connecticut, located, it should be mentioned, at Burton, where such families as the Hitchcocks and Fords—who were both to become prominent in Ohio history—were the pioneers.

The New Connecticut had now representatives of almost every element of population to be found in any part of the country at the opening of the nineteenth century. There were farmers, here as well as in the old Connecticut constituting the truly "respectable" class, and of course the majority of the people; but there were also merchants, mechanics, land speculators, surveyors, the representatives of the law and of medicine, and, as we have seen, of the Church. Yet the people were probably a more homogeneous and truly democratic one than was to be found then or since anywhere on the frontier. A fair edu-

A Conservation of Connecticut

cation was almost universal. Culture was not uncommon. There were a considerable number of college graduates, mostly from Yale; and not alone among these but among the common people it is probable that there existed more knowledge of literature and that more books were to be found than in the midst of any people who had ever journeyed as far as they into the wilds, and by as primitive means. These books were, of course, not numerous save in a relative sense. Beyond the Bible and the New England Primer, Bunyan's Pilgrim's Progress, and Baxter's Saints' Everlasting Rest, Butler's Analogy, Watts on the Mind, and Watts's Hymns seem to have been the mental food of the men of those early days in the western woods. Occasionally the classics or the English poets of the descriptive and didactic schools were to be met with. In nearly every house some books were to be found, and everybody read more or less.

Even the local "character" of the New Connecticut was not an illiterate. Even poor, kindly, wit-wandering Jonathan Chapman, or "Johnny Appleseed," as he was known to all

Ohio and Her Western Reserve

the early residents of the Reserve, not only read, but, it is traditionally affirmed, read Rousseau! A passing tribute must be paid to him who was incidentally the Reserve's first colporteur, but who got his nickname from the perhaps more practical occupation of planting apple-seeds in the wilderness. Surely if he who makes two blades of grass to grow where but one grew before is worthy of praise, much more so was mild-mannered, melancholy, unfortunate "Johnny Appleseed," for he made a million apple-trees to grow where not one was before, and the first orchards of northern Ohio were of trees raised in the several little nurseries that he cleared the ground for and patiently tended without recompense year after year. It was the common belief that this harmless, hapless, weird, but practically altruistic eccentric had lost his reason through a misadventure in love; but, alas! historical investigation ruthlessly calls a check upon imagination, dispels romance, and reveals the hard fact that it was to the less poetic but equally potential cause, the kick of a mule, that poor Johnny's mind was deflected from the normal course. How-

A Conservation of Connecticut

ever it came to him, "Johnny Appleseed's" misfortune was the provocation of frequent discussion among the pioneers of the enigma of good and evil, of predestination, and the doctrines of Calvinistic theology in general. But one result became clear in all the mystery that enveloped his "call." A thousand backwoods farms would have remained long years fruitless but for the strange mania that made him famous.

For the most part the conditions and customs which prevailed during the pioneer times were those which forecast the future, but there were at least two tendencies of the period which fortunately did not become permanent characteristics. These were a marked prevalence and malevolence in the midst of the generally religious community of an assertive, scoffing infidelity, and an enormous consumption of whisky. Both eventually passed without leaving much trace. The first was a part of the license which accompanied the propulsion of the huge wave of liberty from the then recent French Revolution, greatly to the scandal of the godly.

The inordinate use of spirits was more in

Ohio and Her Western Reserve

accordance with the times and conditions of a new country, but it was excessive even for such, and the especial cause is to be found in the fact that poor transportation facilities left the farmers no alternative but to turn their surplus cereals into whisky, which was easily turned elsewhere. The day came when the whole Reserve underwent a revulsion and had to make the mighty effort of the reforming toper. Whisky came into universal use, socially and in private, everywhere, at all times, by all classes—including preachers; was employed in the mechanic arts—such as barn raisings; became the standard of value and medium of exchange, and was employed in almost all transactions. There is, perhaps, no record of a preacher receiving his pay in whisky, but it is well attested that schoolteachers' accounts were thus liquidated, for two young Yankee Puritans (elder brothers of Ohio's great Senator, "Ben" Wade) are mentioned in the records of 1821 as teaching for a few months in the towns of Madison and Monroe and receiving in recompense therefor one six and the other five barrels of whisky.

A Conservation of Connecticut

As the settlements each year dotted the wilderness a little more numerously, the very names written upon its geography were sufficient to denote the nativity of its inhabitants. Not all were Connecticut names, but the majority spoke unerringly of New England origin. The Reserve soon had its Plymouth and its Hartford, its Wyndham and Windsor, its Concord, Amherst, and Andover.

But Connecticut names came to the fore in profusion when the "Sufferers" or "Fire Lands" were surveyed. This region—half a million acres of the extreme western end of the Reserve (now included in the counties of Huron and Erie)—was peopled a little later than the eastern part, but when it did become settled it fairly bristled with historic Connecticut appellations. It was as if the immigrants had combined to emphasize Connecticut here, that there might be no mistake as to where they came from. The Connecticut towns burned by the British in the Revolution—those whose inhabitants were the "Sufferers" here recompensed pound for pound, pence for pence, even to the minutest loss—were New Haven, East Haven, New London, Nor-

Ohio and Her Western Reserve

walk, Greenwich, Fairfield, Danbury, Ridgefield, and Groton. All of these sprang into being in the development of the land scheme, which provided for awards to the fire sufferers, and among them Norwalk became one of the largest towns of "the Fire Lands," as well as one of the most notable in the Reserve for its thrift and beauty—a brilliant Ohio Phœnix arisen from Connecticut ashes.

It is worthy of note that in these "Fire Lands," which perpetuated Connecticut names (and in the greater part of the Reserve), the very manner of survey or subdivision for local government here, as throughout the Reserve, helped to the transplanting of a famous New England institution. The lands were divided into "towns," as they were called in New England, or more properly townships, five miles square, except where the irregular line of the lake shore made "gores" and fractional townships. This regularity and convenience of size was of consequence to the Connecticut people, wonted as they were to the "town meeting," and enabled them to perfect the system and make the "town" a unit of government to a degree which to-day prevails

A Conservation of Connecticut

nowhere else as it does in northern Ohio, save in those States which were the original home of the idea.

As the survey progressed it was found that the entire Reserve of Connecticut, including "the Fire Lands" (500,000 acres), "the Salt Spring Tract" of General Parsons (25,450 acres), Kelley's and the several Bass Islands, lying in the lake off the western end of the

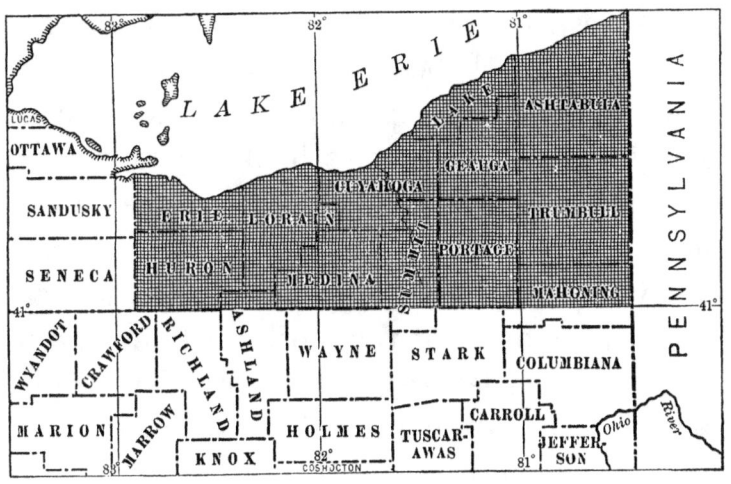

Map showing (by shading) the Western Reserve of Connecticut.

reservation (5,924 acres), contained a total of 3,366,921 acres—an excess over the area of the mother State of 173,921 acres.

Ohio and Her Western Reserve

It may be remarked here that the Reserve includes ten whole counties and fractions of four others, two of which have the bulk of their area in the Reserve. The ten entire counties are Ashtabula, Lake, Geauga, Cuyahoga, Lorain, Huron, Erie, Medina, Portage, and Trumbull. Two-thirds of Mahoning and all but two townships of Summit are in the Reserve, while of two other counties it has small fractions only—three and two townships, respectively, of Ottawa and Ashland.

Enough has been said to show that the New Connecticut reproduced the old. In its zeal for the Church, the school, the college, its people were exhibiting the cherished fondnesses of Connecticut and of New England. They imported the "town meeting," the manners and morals of the mother State. Even in the nomenclature they impressed upon the soil they reared monuments to the memory of their old homes.

The local color of Connecticut prevailed through all of the formative period of the colony's existence. It was patriotic, Presbyterian (or Congregational), Puritanic, yet all of these with a difference, as we shall see presently.

A Conservation of Connecticut

That Connecticut should have been re-created here was only natural from the primal cause that the pioneers were predominantly from Connecticut (though with an intermingling from her sister States). Even in much later years, when a majority of the immigrants came from New York, they were none the less of the same people—the Empire State, in the direct pathway to the West, being but a sojourning-place upon the way, in which an individual might remain a few years or a family for a generation. Scarcely a man among those who early became prominent in the Reserve in statesmanship, literature, the learned professions, or as captains of commerce or industry, but who was native to New England or born of Yankee parents. It was a distinct and homogeneous colony, as direct a progeny of the Puritans as New England itself, and even down to the present, notwithstanding the admixture of a cosmopolitan population, consequent to large growth, it preserves the outward and material characteristics of its original in a more marked manner than does any other community in the whole country.

Ohio and Her Western Reserve

The community owes this circumstance, and the unquestionably great power exerted by its comparatively small population, to two conditions generally recognized by students of sociology, but here perhaps exhibited more unmistakably than elsewhere. In the first place, the pioneers of the New Connecticut, like pretty nearly all pioneers, were the hardiest, the most resolute, and most enterprising of their race; and, secondly, the first born of the pioneers had the benefits, so to speak, of being reared upon a virgin soil, and so adding a new force to old tendencies. It is from this, says Lowell, alluding to the beginnings of States, that men, "like some agricultural products," are produced "better than cultivation can make them afterward. Whether it is in the vigor and freshness which attend the youth of a State, like the youth of a life, or whether such emergencies bring to the surface and into conspicuity a higher order of men—whatever the reason may be, the fact remains, the fathers are larger than the children."

Ancestry and environment, the world-old powerful pair of formative causes, were at

A Conservation of Connecticut

work. The descendants of patriots and Puritans, of preachers, scholars, capable men of affairs, coming early to the new land or born within it, environed by obstacles, but by obstacles which it was possible to overcome through the putting forth of power, and with a broad outlook upon the boundless potentialities that lay in the pure, pristine wilderness to fire their imagination and serve them with incentive, the rugged first comers and first born of the Western Reserve could not fail to perpetuate the principles that had prevailed in the home of their fathers, nor to give them a greater vigor in their own, which was to become the heritage of their sons. The colonists were a peculiarly persistent people, and as they were not called upon here, as at Wyoming, to expend their strength in ceaseless contention, it flowed naturally into the perpetuation of types and the conservation of cherished principles.

Puritanism, Presbyterianism, patriotism formed the triad of the Connecticut settlers' mental equipment of traits and tendencies. But, as has been intimated, these qualities and the general character of the Yankee in

Ohio and Her Western Reserve

the West had undergone considerable of a differentiation from the parent stock.

Curiously, even paradoxically, the community which was the most conservative in the whole western region became also the most progressive, and in fact radical one, in the country. There was perhaps a more bracing breeziness in the moral atmosphere of the south shore of the Lake than on the north shore of the Sound, and this, with the virgin forces of the new country working their mysterious but mighty influences—all brought to bear upon the most vigorous spirits of their race—created a new energy which must have new and enlarged outlets of action.

Puritanism was far too deeply ingrained in these men to fall into disuse as a directing force, but it became a *progressive* Puritanism —vigorous, virile, with the strength of the Young West, to put forth in new-found and multivarious avenues its old-time influence. Here, as of old, Puritanism meant preeminently conscience, and the courage to assert conscience—to act upon it. And here it inspired men, as of old, with unchanged prin-

A Conservation of Connecticut

ciple, but impelled them with irresistible force along absolutely new lines, in new issues.

The church religion of the Connecticut pioneers underwent a similar change, and, while there was no abatement of the piety of the old-time Connecticut Congregationalism, the ancient congealing coldness of Calvinism, as gracefully as it could, yielded to a general softening process, which in part was evident within the denomination, and in some measure went toward the forming of new sects which had been rigorously restrained in the old inflexible social order of the mother State. But while dogma was degraded to something like its proper relative position, and a liberalism prevailed which was looked upon with undisguised horror in Connecticut, and regarded as rank heresy from which naught but evil could ensue, in time those who had abhorred the apostasy of the young western child of the Puritan Yankee were forced to the admission that moral fiber had been wonderfully stiffened even while doctrine had been relaxed. There was thus a revived sectarian religion as well as a new political and social Puritanism, and the practical application of aggressive

Ohio and Her Western Reserve

Christian ethics to newly propounded or newly recognized problems was the inevitable net result.

It was thus that it came about that the Western Reserve was, as early as 1830, a hotbed for the propagation of antislavery sentiment. Charles Backus Storrs, the true pioneer here of advanced learning, as President of Western Reserve College, was inculcating this doctrine of the new conscience as early as 1832, and when he died, two years later, Whittier testified to the esteem in which he was held by the New England abolitionists, in his touching elegy beginning:

> Thou hast fallen in thy armor,
> Thou martyr of the Lord!

Oberlin College, with its new theology, carried on the propaganda of which the lamented Storrs was the pioneer, and Joshua R. Giddings began its battles in Congress when he had no coworker there but John Quincy Adams. The whole Reserve practically became an integral part of the little army which began the battle for freedom and carried it on, with augmented numbers, to its finish. But it was for a long time a curiously

A Conservation of Connecticut

isolated integral of the antislavery army, occupying a position that was advanced (physically and morally) perilously near the frontier of the enemy's country, and performing pioneer duty that demanded the utmost courage. It is not too much to say that the region was the most conspicuous and detested piece of abolition territory in the United States, and that in zeal and accomplishment the Puritans of northern Ohio equaled, if they did not surpass, the Puritans of New England and the Quakers of Pennsylvania. The Reserve unquestionably maintained more stations of the secret "Underground Railroad" than any equal district in the country.

Another exemplification of the new progressivism which had taken hold upon the people was afforded when Oberlin set forth the first exhibit in the world of collegiate coeducation, which she pushed very quickly from tentative experiment to successful exposition, in due time indorsed by the imitation of at least two-thirds of the colleges and universities of the old Northwest, which founded its educational institutions, to a great degree, upon the initiative afforded by the Reserve.

Ohio and Her Western Reserve

But that, with all of their progressiveness, and even radicalism, the Yankee colonists adhered pretty closely to the fundamental principles of the old Puritanism or to a certain broad ethical orthodoxy, must be admitted by the fair-minded observer. For the more ultra "isms" of other "doxies," from first to last, they had little sympathy, and were apt to speedily consign them to that condition in which they were ready for the doxology. Witness, for instance, the short shrift they accorded to Mormonism, transplanted to their soil, flourishing for a time and rearing upon it a costly temple, and yet cast out completely in half a dozen years.

The savor of conscience and courage and of sound morals was in most of the measures which enlisted their sympathies. Seriously speaking, the colonists, like the older Puritans, were a serious people. They had "convictions." And with them convictions amounted almost to organic things. They performed functions in the moral life of these people and were forces in all their greater private and public achievements.

To the older Puritanism the Connecticut

A Conservation of Connecticut

Ohioans added something of humor without abating its earnestness one jot or tittle; but more important than that as a factor in the differentiation was their spirit of spontaneity; and far above all other additions was that shrewd Yankee practicality that they brought to bear in the propagation of their ideals. It was through the exercise of this faculty, coupled with a stern sense of duty and an inherited inability to ignore its dictates, that they entered upon a political fight instead of easefully remaining mere theorists and dreamers, and assisted in the ascendency of a great politico-moral idea.

Puritanism mingled with pure patriotism may be said to have constituted the unwritten but inexorable code of moral aggression on which the great political battles of the mid-century were fought, and they nowhere had fuller sway than here. The old-time Puritanical sense of justice and regard for freedom had come by a marvelous stride in human understanding to include justice and freedom for the man who was black as well as for the man who was white; and from the day that idea dawned on men until the end had been

Ohio and Her Western Reserve

attained, there was no thought in the Western Puritan's mind, with its inflexible sense of duty, but to fight for its realization.

From, and before, the days when Storrs had preached his philippics against slavery at Hudson until freedom was made a political issue under Giddings and Wade—who simply put the old Connecticut Puritan idea of liberty into a new and potent form—the mass of the people were constantly growing more fervent in zeal, until they constituted, unconsciously, an army eager for the fray and only awaiting a commander.

The same slow evolution of forces to which Thomas Hooker, Puritan preacher of Connecticut, had given an initial impulse in 1638 had by 1850 wrought the mass of Reserve citizens to a realizing sense of the iniquity of slavery, and by the operation of happy laws of heredity those who were to be the captains in the country-wide contest had been slowly preparing for their great work. The deep but silent, smoldering conviction of the former was finally aroused and organized for action by the fulminating words of the latter, which ultimately fired the whole country.

A Conservation of Connecticut

But long before that result was reached the society of Puritan pioneers found itself marked with a peculiar and proud distinction. The virile, uncompromising moral and political spirit of the people, as it began to exercise its destined dominance, provoked from their opponents of the press and stump the sneering assertion that the Connecticut Reserve was "a State separate from Ohio." It did virtually constitute a separate State, or the equal of a State, in sovereignty and in splendid isolation—a State in all save actual organization. Its people had come to possess and exert a power, probably, in proportion to their numbers, greater than any other in the nation, certainly greater than any in the West, and more than any other of their relatively small number they impressed the conscience and swayed the destiny of the nation. From the time of the Free-Soil movement to the close of the antislavery fight the Western Reserve of Connecticut was a literal fortress of freedom and an exhaustless base of supply for the battle at the front.

The early leaders of this Western Puritan force in its fight for freedom, the greatest men

Ohio and Her Western Reserve

whom the Reserve contributed to the service of the nation—Joshua Reed Giddings and Benjamin Franklin Wade—were perfect types of the Puritan pioneer society of which they became the political representatives. As such it is interesting to glance at their antecedents and achievements; for all that has been said of the influence of ancestry and of moral idea —of the persistence of Puritanism in the class—finds forceful confirmation and apt illustration in their individual careers.

Giddings and Wade, the twin giants of the Reserve, were of one backwoods county, which they brought into national fame—huge Ashtabula, the political Gibraltar of the Western abolitionists. These two stanch, unpolished statesmen were partners in the profession of law, lifelong friends, colleagues in Congress, one as Representative, the other as Senator. Their origins and early experiences were very like those of thousands of the early comers to the Puritan colony. They had histories strangely similar to each other, and they were typical of the times and the land they lived in. Both were of the Puritan patriot stock and of distinguished lineage, as

A Conservation of Connecticut

ancient almost as the settlement of New England would admit. The Giddings family progenitor immigrated to Massachusetts in 1635, and removed to Lyme, Conn., less than a century later. Their genealogy shows service by some members in the French and Indian War, the Revolution, the War of 1812, and the war for the Union, and it reveals the names of distinguished Americans, such as Rufus Choate and Nathaniel Hawthorne. The parents of Joshua R. Giddings were very early Connecticut settlers in Pennsylvania, and it was there—at Tioga Point—that he was born, in 1795. Eleven years later he was brought to the newly opened Reserve, near the site of Jefferson, which was destined to become famous jointly as his and "Ben" Wade's home.

JOSHUA R. GIDDINGS.

Wade, like Giddings, was of very old family, the first American forbear becoming a resident of Medford, Mass., in 1632. It takes

Ohio and Her Western Reserve

nature a long time to make a man of Benjamin Franklin Wade's stature, and evoluting protoplasm and mysterious mind pass by many strange meanders to perform the function. Massive, rugged, a warrior born, if ever there was one, Wade had strains of blood from two poets—gentle Anne Dudley Bradstreet, daughter of Governor Dudley, born 1612, the famous "Tenth Muse" and first poetess of America; and austere, profoundly puritanic Michael Wigglesworth, whose quaintly dismal and abysmal Day of Doom gave Cotton Mather pious delight, which he evinced by prophesying that it "would be read in New England until its pictures were realized by the event." The Dudleys were a great people in the history of old England and of New England, and so were the Uphams, who contributed to the molding of the Yankee Puritan Ohio Senator, while the Wades themselves were not wanting in honor or fame, for several of them were officers in the patriot army, and one a privateer of most remarkable adventures. Of the complex yet homogeneously Puritan and patriot blood, the son of poets and fighters, Benjamin Franklin Wade was

A Conservation of Connecticut

born at "Feeding Hills," now in Springfield, Mass., in the year 1800. He was next to the youngest of eleven children, the younger brother, beside himself the only one destined to fame, being Edward Wade the future Congressman. "Ben" Wade, or "Frank," as he was commonly called at his Ohio home, and Edward Wade came to the Reserve in 1821.

There, in Ashtabula County, and eventually in Jefferson, its seat of justice, became united in fast fellowship of political convictions and general intellectual sympathy the lives of the two strongest men of their time in the Western Reserve. They were

BENJAMIN FRANKLIN WADE.

not the first, but they were the foremost of a succession of men of ability which this Connecticut settlement sent to Congress. One, at least, and probably both of them were students at that famous old-time private law school of the region which graduated many great lawyers and several statesmen—the law

Ohio and Her Western Reserve

office of Whittlesey & Newton, at Canfield, in Mahoning County. The senior of this firm of perhaps the ablest lawyers in the whole settlement, Elisha Whittlesey, had already entered Congress—he served from 1823 to 1838—and Eben Newton went later.

Giddings succeeded Whittlesey in the House of Representatives in 1838, and began that wonderful career of twenty-one years in Congress, in which, when the mantle of the dying John Quincy Adams fell upon his shoulders in 1840, he became, and remained for a decade, the preeminent leader of the antislavery forces in the House. The end toward which his unceasing and herculean labors tended was freedom; and the means by which that end was attained can be more justly attributed to his foreseeing sagacity than to any other single personal cause. He laid down the principle on which the Free-Soil party planted itself in 1848, and embodied it in the Republican platform of 1856 in the resolution declaring the extension of slavery unconstitutional. This was the fundamental article of faith, and of ultimate force, upon which organized political action

A Conservation of Connecticut

against slavery was started, and that authority upon our political history, Von Holst, testifies that "to Giddings more than to any other person belongs the credit of having with full consciousness made it the constitutional basis of the entire warfare against the slave power, and of having applied it with a consistency never before attained, to all questions to which it was pertinent."

Wade supplemented in the Senate the great work of Giddings in the House, coming into the battle in its heat and remaining long enough to be gratified by the complete victory—which was not permitted to Giddings. He served continuously for eighteen years (1851–'69), and became President of the Senate., But a prouder distinction than that was his in being second only to Giddings in the struggle for freedom. In some respects he was his superior.

Neither of these men, it must be noted, were great orators in the true meaning of the term, though both sometimes arose to heights of eloquence which might fairly entitle them to be so classed. Their immense power and momentous achievement must be accredited

Ohio and Her Western Reserve

to the burning earnestness of their convictions, their indomitable spirit, and irresistible aggressiveness. To this must be added the intelligence and the temper of their constituencies, which, with that intense, vital practicality (heretofore alluded to as the Western pioneers' paramount addition to Puritanism), persisted in keeping men once proved able and honest at the front of the fight as their champions—a sapient policy, by the way, not to be underestimated as a factor in the political prestige not only of the Western Reserve, but of the State of Ohio.

Both Giddings and Wade represented the best of New England. The mind and morals of Puritanism and an exalted patriotism found convincing utterance through their personalities. But they were as representative of the pioneers—as good examples of the potentiality of the "plain people"—as they were of New England. Their education was of the backwoods, and their gigantic growth of physical and moral stature was gained there. They could handle the rifle with the accuracy of experts, and they learned to fell trees before they studied Blackstone. Giddings

A Conservation of Connecticut

chopped wood and split rails, like Abraham Lincoln, and Wade worked on the Erie Canal, as Garfield did upon that in Ohio. Both were stately, stalwart men, six feet or more in stature, whose every motion displayed power of mind and body. Both were morally made up from the full trinity of ancestral influences, supplemented by Western vigor and radicalism. They had alike the New England genius for general reform, recognized its new needs in the West, and both came early to oppose alcoholic intemperance, as they did slavery, when the doctrine was exceedingly unpopular.

The graves of these two friends, constant companions, coworkers, as they were through life, fittingly lie close together in the little cemetery of the green and quiet village of Jefferson, which their lives and works made historic ground. Relics of the two fearless, sturdy statesmen abound in the town. Their quaint old law offices are preserved, and these and the graves of Giddings and Wade are alike the Mecca of pilgrimages of grateful gray-headed black men who were one time slaves, and of reverent readers of history.

Ohio and Her Western Reserve

Something of the powerful personality of these heroic men seems still to pervade the shaded and hushed streets where once they walked. The very quietude and simplicity of the surroundings conforms to the character of the men who fared forth from this rural village; but what a contrast it suggests to the stern strenuousness of their careers and the resounding clash of conflict they brought about! They were not the mere pioneers of a place and people, but the resolute pioneers of a vast moral revolution. Yet, practically, the training of these warriors of world-wide fame had its inception here in one of the obscurest villages of a young colony. They were the greatest product of the Connecticut Reserve, and its greatest gift to the nation. It was through them that the distinctive character of the colony made its chief impress upon the country and gained public fame. Reflection upon their achievement and their influence in molding the national mind compels appreciation of the enormous significance of the settlement and the truest triumph of Connecticut in the West.

These men represented a terribly strong

A Conservation of Connecticut

and yet a morally restrained radicalism; but John Brown, also of the Reserve, a fierce and fanatical radicalism. He, whom Fate hurled, a human firebrand, to light the actual and consuming conflagration in the already smoking flax, was brought here from Connecticut as a child of five years, and it was from here that he and his sons went into "bleeding Kansas," and he, ultimately, to that death which has given him in history an equivocal position between hero and fanatic.

CHAPTER VII

THE RESERVE'S CONTRIBUTIONS TO PUBLIC SERVICE

NOTHING denotes more decidedly than its relatively large number of famous men the intellectual energy of a community. As the old Connecticut was made conspicuous in the first half of the nineteenth century by the multitude of its prominent men (as is set forth in Chapter I), so the New Connecticut became noted in later generations for its prolific production of men who became notable as lawyers, legislators, statesmen, soldiers, authors, educators, scientists, inventors; and thus, in this respect, as in many others, asserted herself the most worthy daughter of a wonderful mother State.

There were other Congressmen than Wade and Giddings in the Reserve's list who shed luster upon it and performed valuable service for the nation. Jacob Brinkerhoff, the fore-

Contributions to Public Service

runner of a family conspicuous in Ohio, and one of the very few not of New England origin, but of Hollandish and Huguenot stock for many generations in America, came early to Plymouth, on the extreme southern border of the Reserve, and as a Congressman from 1843 to 1847 assisted the work of a Connecticut-Pennsylvania colleague, David Wilmot, the original draft of whose famous "proviso" he drew. A relative, Henry R. Brinkerhoff, went to Congress from one of the western counties of the Reserve; but more noted of those from that region were Eleutheros Cooke, Joseph M. Root, and James Monroe, of Oberlin. Among those from the eastern and middle districts there should not pass unmentioned Peter Hitchcock, Elisha Whittlesey, Jonathan Sloan, Sherlock J. Andrews, Edward Wade, Sidney Edgerton, John Hutchins, Albert Gallatin Riddle, Rufus P. Spalding, William H. Upson, Ezra B. Taylor, Tom L. Johnson, and Stephen A. Northaway. Of Senators not otherwise mentioned there are the pioneer Harley Griswold, the latter-time Henry B. Payne, and, latest of all, Marcus Alonzo Hanna.

Ohio and Her Western Reserve

James A. Garfield, it must also be borne in mind, was a long-time Congressman, and for a very short period Senator, before he was President. This typical man of the Reserve, who turned the eyes of the whole nation toward it, like Wade and Giddings, of the long-lined New England stock from Massachusetts, Connecticut, and New Hampshire, was born at Orange, educated (in part) at Hiram, and went to the White House from Mentor. William McKinley, the second President of the United States furnished by the Reserve, like Garfield long time a Congressman, was born at Niles.

Then, too, among men of note who have entered the halls of national legislation from other States, but who had earlier homes in the Reserve, there should be mentioned Senator and, earlier, Representative, Bishop W. Perkins, who succeeded Preston B. Plumb, from Kansas; Senator John P. Jones, of Nevada; Congressman Horr, of Michigan, who emigrated from the western, and Senator Julius Cæsar Burrows, of the same State, from the eastern, portion of the Reserve (who left two brothers of not less ability and of equally

Contributions to Public Service

classic names in his old home). It may be remarked *en passant* that the apportionment will only admit of a very minute percentage of those natives of the Reserve who have the requisite ability entering Congress directly from this phenomenally favored region, and so some of the most aspiring must seek less crowded, if more roundabout, paths by way of other localities. Altogether, the Reserve has supplied the nation with two Presidents, five Senators, and its full complement of Congressmen, besides members of the Cabinet, foreign ministers, and United States district judges. When it is borne in mind that the Reserve is but little more than one-seventh of the State of Ohio, it will be seen that she has supplied men of national note in excess even of the large proportion for which Ohio has deservedly held high repute.

But her contributions to the civil roster of the State have been scarcely less important and indicative of her prominence as an integral part of the commonwealth than have those to the nation. She has furnished a full score of its Supreme Court judges, among them perhaps more than her share of Chief Justices

Ohio and Her Western Reserve

(of whom one not heretofore mentioned was Judge Rufus P. Ranney, a jurist of national reputation), and no less than six chief executives, including the "war Governors." Of these the pioneer Samuel Huntington—to whom tribute has already been paid—was her first. He was the second elected Governor of the State, and served from 1808 to 1810. Later came Seabury Ford (1848-'49), and Reuben Wood (1850-'51), both, like Huntington, New Englanders. When the war broke out David Tod, of the old Connecticut settlement of Youngstown, was elected Governor in the autumn of 1861, and gave the State an efficient administration, which made it one of the strong forces in the prosecution of the war. In the campaign of 1863 another candidate from the Reserve was put forward —John Brough, a native, indeed, of that other New England settlement, Marietta, but then a resident of Cleveland, a "war Democrat," who had years before been a popular and powerful leader, and he was triumphantly elected over Vallandigham. Brough died in the summer of 1865, and was succeeded by the Lieutenant-Governor; but at the fall

Contributions to Public Service

election still another Western Reserve candidate was put forward in the late Major-General Jacob Dolson Cox, who was essentially a "war Governor," though after war time. The most distinguished Ohio soldier who went into the war without military education or experience (whose close second was Garfield, also a major-general from civil life) was overwhelmingly elected, and was the sixth representative of the Connecticut corner of the State in the executive office. Later, General Cox was Secretary of the Interior in President Grant's first Cabinet, and still later a member of Congress.

If we pursue the list of civil war generals contributed by the Reserve we find that, besides Garfield and Cox, there were the two Paines—Halbert E. and Eleazar A. (the latter a graduate of West Point)—both major-generals, Q. A. Gillmore, Russell A. Alger, Emerson Opdyke, Joel A. Dewey, and J. W. Reilly.

But not alone in politics, statesmanship, and martial glory have the matron's jewels shone. The domains of literature and art and the department of education and general culture in the country at large have received re-

Ohio and Her Western Reserve

peatedly the impetus of some reenforcement from the intellectually fresh and fecund Western Reserve, though in the latter cause it may perhaps be admitted that she has done more for her own sons and daughters than for those of her neighbors.

As the child of Connecticut who could find no better use for the price paid for the lands of this district than to devote it to her public schools, it was natural that the young Connecticut should foster education. She did so from the outstart. Not only the common schools, but institutions of higher learning sprang up with surprising quickness, and flourished with astonishing vigor, in some cases, to most gratifying fruition.

Of several academies in the new settlement, one developed into Western Reserve College, located at Hudson. The germ was planted in 1803, and the college came into existence in 1826. The strong predilection of the people was expressed in the pet patronymic bestowed upon this institution—"the Yale of the West"—and that, too, defined the aim and ambition of its founders. It attained dignity and thoroughness, and with a

Contributions to Public Service

faculty containing from the first some famous educators soon became an institution of considerable worth in developing culture and character in the New Connecticut.

It was preeminently the college of the first-born of the pioneers, and many of the more well-to-do and aspiring among them laid there the foundations for future usefulness and success. It put forth at an early day a medical department, which obtained wide recognition. This was planted in Cleveland, to which city the entire institution, now known as the Western Reserve University—of which Adelbert College, nobly endowed, is the chief factor—was removed in 1882. An exception from the first to the rule that small colleges are feeble and sorry institutions, it has constantly risen toward ideal standards as it has increased in attendance and general prosperity. A great impetus was given its ascendancy by the reorganization effected under Rev. H. C. Haydn, and now under the presidency of Rev. Charles F. Thwing it has perhaps a thousand students, a large faculty containing many educators of more than local note, and a noble library, with all de-

Ohio and Her Western Reserve

partments housed in stately, scholastic architecture. But in one respect it remains unchanged since it was the Yale of the pioneers' sons: although unsectarian, a great preponderance of its students are of the Presbyterian and Congregational faiths, which prevailed among their fathers.

As we have already seen, it was an early president of this college who was the pioneer of antislavery agitation in the West. The institution became famous largely through his radicalism, but the marked ability of its faculty also contributed to its repute. Many of its members attained distinction there or elsewhere, Laurens P. Hickok, its first Professor of Theology, becoming President of Union College, New York, and others being called to the larger Eastern colleges.

Hiram and Wooster—the former known principally to fame through the presidency of that sound scholar the late Burke A. Hinsdale, D. D., subsequently of Michigan University, and the fact that it was the school which Garfield attended; and the latter kept in the minds of men by its medical department, rivaling in Cleveland that of the Western Re-

Contributions to Public Service

serve—were two more meritorious institutions which attested the zeal of the young colony in education.

Oberlin came into being, and still stands for an idea about equally embodied in town and college, both rather curiously created and maintained by one force. It had its origin in 1833 in an evangelistic movement, and may be regarded as an extra-condensed concretion, or crystallization, of the ultra-radical religious element in the Reserve, just as "the Yale of the West" was of the more conservative mind. Oberlin carried coeducation to a convincing success with a rush, and it may be looked upon as demonstrating equally well another coeducation than that combining the sexes— a coeducation in Congregationalism and secular science. It represents radicalism in practical application (even to the prohibition of tobacco), the most marked demonstration of which was in the old-time abolition movement and its service as a station of the "Underground Railroad." It affords a liberal training to thousands—it has about 1,400 students—and sends them into the world as well equipped with religious and philosoph-

Ohio and Her Western Reserve

ical ideas of the "benevolent theory" as with more worldly knowledge. Its great names were those of Finney and Keep—Rev. Charles G. Finney and "Father" John Keep—but its greatest that of ex-President James Harris Fairchild, all of New England, and the last-named probably the foremost educator of the Western Reserve.

Of the other advanced educational institutions, Lake Erie College, founded at Painsville, in 1856, for the education of young women, is peculiarly of New England initiative, being the eldest daughter of Mount Holyoke. Besides all these, there is Buchtel College at Akron, Baldwin and German Wallace at Berea, and various normal and special schools, as the Case School of Applied Science, in Cleveland.

Education flourished so well on the fresh, strong soil to which it was transplanted that some of the best seed was carried back to replenish the old garden from whence the stock came, or, to change the metaphor, a reflex tide set in, and Connecticut, which had long supplied teachers for her colony, some years ago began to receive them from it. The

Contributions to Public Service

Western Reserve became a recruiting ground, and Western Reserve University, especially, a recruiting station, for the faculty of Yale. George Trumbull Ladd, D. D., LL. D., who a score of years ago became identified with Yale, and is now its Professor of Psychology, went from Painesville, where he was born, and though not indeed by way of the university mentioned, he was probably the pioneer of the native-born in reverse movement from West to East, and to his success may be attributed Yale's predilection for Ohio professors. He enjoys a world-wide reputation, and has lately been made the recipient of unusual honors in Japan, India, and other far countries. His is perhaps the subtlest mind the Western Reserve has contributed to the educational world and the domain of pure thought.

Even the common schools of the New Connecticut are of uncommon excellence. President Eliot, of Harvard, has commended those of Cleveland as an example worthy the emulation of Boston. Those throughout the Reserve are equally well organized and conducted.

Ohio and Her Western Reserve

The Rev. I. Jennings was the author of what was known (from the place of his residence) as "the Akron plan," which was applied eventually to the schools of the whole State, and, indeed, of numerous other States; and Hon. Harvey Rice, of Cleveland, from his zeal in forwarding its adoption by the Legislature, became popularly known as the "Father of the Ohio School System."

HON. THOMAS W. HARVEY.

But it was to another resident of the Reserve, the late Thomas W. Harvey, more than to any other single citizen, that the schools of Ohio came to owe the elevation of their standard and that general effectiveness of system which gave them fame even in Boston! A New Hampshire Yankee who looked like the ideal German professor and had the poise of a Greek philosopher, nearly the whole of his long life was spent as a superintendent of several favored schools of the Re-

Contributions to Public Service

serve until his fitness for the position, long masked by modesty, led to his election as State school superintendent. He was the author, too, of text-books used in half the States of the Union, and altogether the most useful and popular educator which the region ever supplied to the common-school system of the State.

To the literature of the country, it may be briefly said, the Reserve has probably contributed far more than its quota of authors, and among them several of first rank. One of the first, in a chronological sense at least, was curiously enough a woman, and one not usually accredited to the Reserve or to the West—Delia Salter Bacon, born at Tallmadge, 1811, the original exponent of the theory of the Baconian authorship of the poems and dramas usually ascribed to one William Shakespeare.

Albert Gallatin Riddle, lawyer and member of Congress, formed a connecting link between statesmanship and author-craft, and to him must be given the title of the novelist *of* the Western Reserve, while Howells will, of course, be acclaimed the leading fictionist

Ohio and Her Western Reserve

and general man of letters *from* the same favored region. Riddle's Bart Ridgley and The Portrait will live at least in the land they vividly picture.

William Dean Howells is inseparably associated with the town of Jefferson (where his father, also an author, spent most of his life), and upon the mere mention of his name some suggestion of his easeful grace, his gentleness and literary geniality, merges with the sterner memories of the rugged statesman who lived there. As if in apprehension of a possibility that some few souls in the whole round world of fiction lovers should not rise to the refined realism of the Reserve's first literary artist, the same county which contributed Howells to the country kindly made it a present of antipodal character in Edward S. Ellis, the father of the dime novel and of many better things.

Miss Edith Thomas, most classic of all

Contributions to Public Service

our women singers, comes also from Ashtabula County. So, too, do Judge Albion W. Tourgee, Thomas Jay Hudson, and Ambrose Bierce.

But other sections of the Reserve have not been without literary light—and lights. The late Prof. Burke A. Hinsdale was as eminent an author as educator, and labored to good effect in controversial, critical, and historical lines of literature. General Jacob Dolson Cox obtained fame as a writer upon the civil war, as well as an actor in it, and Prof. George Trumbull Ladd, of Yale, conjoins authorship with college duties.

James Ford Rhodes, author of that monumental work The History of the United States from the Compromise of 1850, which, as it has progressed through four large octavo volumes, has revealed rare judicial qualities as well as brilliancy of style, is of Cleveland birth and New England parentage. Sarah C. Woolsey, better known as "Susan Coolidge," was born and spent her youth in the same city, and the latter clause is true of Sarah Knowles Bolton. Constance Fenimore Woolson's whole literary life was also

Ohio and Her Western Reserve

spent there, as was also most of that of John Hay before literature suffered a loss that diplomacy might derive a gain. George Kennan, of Russian travels fame, was born at Norwalk. G. Frederick Wright, author as well as scientist, and the breezy Alfred Henry Lewis, are among those who claim the Reserve as birthplace.

In the realm of art there are fewer eminent names to boast, but they are not totally lacking. James H. and William H. Beard, the famous painters (who made animals the medium of subtlest satires of men), were originally of Painesville and the sons of David Beard, of the surveying party of 1796. Among younger artists who call the Reserve home, probably the best known is Kenyon Cox, born at Warren; and Frederick Opper, the cartoonist, comes from Madison.

If we seek to chronicle the names of those

JAY COOKE.

Contributions to Public Service

other men of the Reserve whose lights have shone for the nation or the whole world, our task becomes too great. At most only a few can be mentioned of the many who have fame, but the list must include first of all the veteran financier Jay Cooke — the Robert Morris of the rebellion —born in Sandusky, in 1821, and the latest survivor of all the Ohioans who were of the first rank of usefulness in the period of the civil war. Mr. Cooke then, and ever since, a citizen of Philadelphia, financed the Federal operations to the amount of $2,000,000,000, raising funds where others failed, and thus making possible the successful prosecution of the war. There were also those twin masters of electricity, Thomas A. Edison and Charles F. Brush, born respectively at Milan and Euclid; Platt R. Spencer, the inventor of the Spencerian system of writing;

Thomas A. Edison

Ohio and Her Western Reserve

and such scientists as Jared P. Kirtland, John Strong Newberry, Charles Whittlesey, and G. Frederick Wright.

Thus the Western Reserve is shown to have become a community of which the outgoings, rather than the incomings, are now of paramount concern. She gives more than she receives.

Cleveland, her metropolis, which had only seven souls in 1800, had by the middle of the century—largely owing to the location of the Ohio Canal terminus there, through the agency of Alfred Kelley—a population of over 25,000; in 1860, 43,838; in 1870, 92,829; in 1880, 160,146; in 1890, 261,353; and in 1900 reached 381,768.

But not alone in numbers is the accumulated strength of this people to be expressed. Men like Henry Chisholm and Joseph Perkins gave it the initials of impetus which, continued by others, have created a lake commerce five-sixths as large as the entire coastwise and foreign commerce of New York, which is 12,000,000 tons per year, and have made it in ship-building (if the construction of war-vessels at Philadelphia be excepted

Contributions to Public Service

from the computation) second only in the whole world to the Clyde. And these same men, and others, as Leonard Case, J. H. Wade, and Amasa Stone, by their munificence have adorned the city with college buildings, libraries, and parks, so that grateful evidences of philanthropic expenditure are as conspicuous as the gigantic commercial apparatus for the getting of gain.

Cleveland long ago passed beyond the possibility of being properly compared with the chief city of Connecticut. She is not the New Haven, nor the Hartford, but the Boston of the West—Boston-like in the conservatism of her financial institutions, in her commercial vigor, her character and culture.

But if Cleveland has its prototype in Boston, its environing Western Reserve still presents the moral contour and color of the mother State. Bearing in mind the fact that it is about 175,000 acres, or, say, a couple of thousand farms, larger than Connecticut, and knowing that it has as a whole kept fairly apace with its metropolis in population, one is not surprised to find it only lacking about 9,000 of the 700,000 mark in 1890, and reach-

Ohio and Her Western Reserve

ing in 1900 the round number of 884,445, which comes within a few thousands of the population of Connecticut. Thus while only a fraction—scarcely more than a seventh—of the big Buckeye State, the New Connecticut surpasses in people several of the important commonwealths. It has fully four times as many as little Delaware, more than twice as many as Rhode Island or Vermont or New Hampshire, while it handsomely exceeds the great State of Maine and almost equals the population of West Virginia.

It becomes thus apparent that in numbers, commercial importance, geographical extent —in all save mere formal organization—the Connecticut Western Reserve constitutes the equivalent of a State; while in its unity of purpose and power of influence it has unquestionably exercised in the affairs of the nation and in the broad interests of the people a sway such as few States, large or little, have equaled.

It is in this achievement, in the perpetuation of principles and of an individual character as complete as if bounded by State lines, or lofty mountains and wide rivers, and in the

Contributions to Public Service

unquestioned fact that more than any other similar body of people west of the Alleghenies it "has impressed the brain and conscience of the country," that the perseverance of the Connecticut colonists who planted Wyoming and were for a half century militant in Pennsylvania was finally rewarded and rendered triumphant in Ohio. Persistent dream of colonial expansion had never in our history more palpable, if less theatric, realization in more peaceful conquest.

"What constitutes a State?
Not high rais'd battlement or labored mound,
Thick wall or moated gate;
Not cities proud with spires and turrets crowned;
Not bays and broad armed ports,
Where, laughing at the storm, rich navies ride;
Not starr'd and spangled courts
Where low browed baseness wafts perfumes to pride.
No : Men, high-minded men.
. . . .
Men, who their duties know,
But know their rights and knowing dare maintain,
Prevent the long-aimed blow,
And crush the tyrant, while they rend the chain,
These constitute a State."
Sir William Jones (1746–1794).

States are not great
Except as men make them;
Men are not great except they do and dare;
But States, like men,
Have destinies that take them—
That bear them on, not knowing why or where.
Eugene F. Ware.

CHAPTER VIII

OHIO AND THE "GREAT ORDINANCE" OF 1787

THAT commonwealth into whose unorganized territory Connecticut, by the most energetic and momentous movement of internal expansion that the Western world ever witnessed, thrust six hundred miles from her own borders, the largest distinct organized colony to be found in the whole nation, has now rounded a century of statehood. By reason of that fact, because, too, of many conjoining links between them, because both of certain similarities and contrasts in their histories, it becomes appropriate, if not imperative, to chronicle here some of the essentials of her curious origin and great career.

The reader is asked, therefore, to pass from the comparatively simple story of one people in three States to the consideration of the more complicated study of many peoples

Ohio and Her Western Reserve

in one State—a State historically the most cosmopolitan in the Union and absolutely unique in the entire aggregation, as to origin, upbuilding, and influence.

Ohio, which leaped from nothingness to third place in the Union in the brief space of forty years, and held that position for half a century, has furnished Chief Executives for the United States for a total period of more than twenty years, and furthermore it has contributed legislators, jurists, soldiers, statesmen neither in number, influence, nor general value of public service secondary to those of any State in the sisterhood, while it has been also one of the stanchest bulwarks for the preservation of our political integrity, and one of the strongest agencies for our material prosperity.

A swift survey of the means through which the remarkable ascendency of this State in the affairs of the nation was attained, through the wise and fortuitous laying of her foundations, together with a recounting of some of its important services for the nation, will reveal a plexus of causes for the prestige the State possesses fully as interesting to con-

FORT HARMAR.

On the Ohio River, at the mouth of the Muskingum, built 1785-'86.

The "Great Ordinance" of 1787

template as is the net result to which they have tended.

Looking backward from the vantage-point of what has been accomplished, it is easy to detect what were the chief formative influences in the projection of the State. As is everywhere apparent in political retrospects, one will readily see that in this instance while many of the means by which the State arrived at its peculiar prominence have been what must be called adventitious ones—the inexorable flow of a great group of beneficent results from fixed and favoring causes, uninfluenced by the wisdom or the action of man—others are traceable to the sagacity of statesmen (of the early Union and to some extent of the State) and the general diffusion of a high intelligence among the people at large—the citizens of the State.

To say that the causes of this commonwealth's healthful growth to prosperity and robust usefulness were various, is to repeat one of the veriest commonplaces of history. But the happy conjunction of causes, the conspiring of diverse influences of man and nature, toward a single end, has rarely had so perfect

Ohio and Her Western Reserve

an illustration in the whole field of history as that which Ohio's founding and development affords. Geographical conditions and the greed of man supplemented the far-seeing and unselfish measures of patriots. If there are "psychological moments" in the lives of nations as well as in those of men, one of those moments or periods must have been seized for the movement which resulted in Ohio. Its settlement projected by patriots under the personal counsel of Washington; its fundamental law conceived in a spirit which seemed almost superhuman in its farseeing (though its adoption was accomplished by very human craft); reaching statehood largely through the urgent political necessities of the new Jeffersonian Democracy; its population contributed to in the first flush of their independence and new-found strength by the people of the whole nation—every episode of the times favored, and it seemed almost as if the very elements themselves fostered its beginnings, and indeed, as if all nature was especially lubricated for the occasion of this origin, as was fitting enough should be the case, for the launching of such a ship of State.

The "Great Ordinance" of 1787

The Ordinance of Freedom, or the Ordinance of 1787, was, of course, the great favoring first cause in the destiny of Ohio (as well as of the four other States of the old Northwest Territory to which it equally applied). This, too, was the first and chief of those formative causes operating on Ohio, which involved thought, foresight, purpose, and ultimately distinguished Ohio as a State very different from the sporadic growths lying to the southward. Kentucky and Tennessee may be said, like Topsy, to have "just growed." They were resultant simply from the vague, aimless, undirected and lawless individual pioneerings of the Virginian and Carolinian people. But Ohio had parents. It had progenitors, projectors. It was the child of purpose. Its career was most kindly conserved and promoted by destiny and by fortuitous circumstance, but it owed much to good birth. The Ordinance of 1787 clothed the soil with law before the footprint of an authorized settler fell upon it.

The establishment of freedom forever in the Northwest Territory, through the Ordinance of 1787, has employed hundreds of

Ohio and Her Western Reserve

able pens, and never ceases to be the favorite theme for eloquent tongues; but another phase of the operation of the great ordinance paramount to its prohibition of slavery seldom or never receives its proper meed of praise. And this is a vital one in the consideration of Ohio's foundation and upbuilding. Let the student who seeks to understand Ohio first of all come to a realization of the fact that in the prohibition of slavery from the territory northwest of the Ohio River *the ordinance became the agency for the selection of the people* who were to ultimately settle that vast land— and earliest of all Ohio. The prohibition of slavery within the territory was, of course, an emphatic exclusion of the slaveholder, but it was an equally emphatic invitation to all those, whether of North or South, who opposed slavery. And that meant the men of firmest moral stamina in the whole country, especially the South—the men who morally and politically were three-quarters of a century in advance of their fellows.

This is a topic which will be hereafter reverted to for the sake of some specific proof and illustration of the effective working of the

The "Great Ordinance" of 1787

measure in the matter alluded to; but in this connection it must suffice to say that the manner in which through the passing years the Ordinance of Freedom went on its work of sifting from the whole country the primal population of Ohio marks its greatest service to the State. It is as a stupendous moral engine, working automatically, silently, with ceaseless strength, through a long period, almost as perfectly as nature's own inflexible law of evolution, for the formation of a State by selection of the best from all States, that we must view the ordinance in its mighty, molding force upon Ohio, and finally upon the nation. A far broader effect, of course, the ordinance had in its bearings upon the destiny of the country at large. It prepared the way by making the great Northwest free-soil territory for the overthrow of slavery in America, virtually deciding the battle before the birth of the soldiers who fought it. But the fact remains that it was more specifically in the ways here set forth that it affected the State which forms the subject of present consideration, and of whose phenomenal planting and rise in the sisterhood of States it

Ohio and Her Western Reserve

was *the first humanly planned and purposed cause.*

The ordinance, which was really the constitution of the old Northwest Territory, and marked its legal beginning, was the culmination of a long series of endeavors in the direction of wise and beneficent measures tending toward the nationalization of the West, involving the deepest concern of the leading statesmen of the time, and vying in momentousness with the formation of the Union itself. To Maryland is due the credit for the initial movement, or what one searching student of history has called " the pioneer thought," in regard to the nationalization of the lands northwest of the Ohio, ultimately accomplished by the cession of State claims. Then came the consideration of providing for and planting government in the domain thus vested in the nation. Four ordinances had been brought before Congress in turn, and finally one had been passed, after the expiration of three years; but even that was a nullity, and was ultimately repealed by the Ordinance of Freedom.

This came into force with surprising sud-

The "Great Ordinance" of 1787

denness after the long and tedious delays and the successive failures of the preceding measures. Why? Because a land company had been formed in New England—the Ohio Land Company—the outgrowth of a conference at the close of the War of Independence, in 1783, between General Jedediah Huntington and General Rufus Putnam; and the agent of this company was offering to purchase a large body of lands—1,500,000 acres—northwest of the Ohio and plant there a colony, if Congress would enact such legislation for the territory as would be satisfactory to the proposing purchasers.

This agent, the Rev. Manasseh Cutler, LL. D., of Ipswich, Mass., Congregational clergyman, got into his gig, and rolling leisurely down to New York, accomplished in one week what had baffled others for three years. He secured the passage of the immortal ordinance on July 13, 1787.

Rev. MANASSEH CUTLER.

Ohio and Her Western Reserve

As to the authorship of the document, now very generally claimed for him, it was probably a composite labor. He wrote some portions of it. So also very likely did Nathan Dane, for whom Webster claimed the authorship, and Rufus King; so, too, perhaps Richard Henry Lee and William Grayson. Thomas Jefferson had much to do with it, or rather with a former and in some respects similar ordinance, which had contained a clause for the ultimate prohibition of slavery, but which had failed of passage.

Whatever the doubts concerning Cutler's authorship of the ordinance, it is incontestable that he was the agent who secured its passage, and that, too, with its clause absolutely, and from the date of enactment, prohibiting slavery, whereas the great influence of Jefferson had been insufficient to secure the passage of a far weaker one not long previously. The truth was the Rev. Manasseh Cutler was a prince of diplomats and the pioneer of lobbyists, and he had a strong cause to plead before a body so favorably disposed toward the acceptance of his general proposition — so keenly alive to the benefits that would accrue

The "Great Ordinance" of 1787

to the country through its acceptance—that they were willing to make some concessions to insure its carrying out. The company he represented was composed almost entirely of New England officers of the patriot army, 288 in number, all personally known to Washington and generally to the Congress and country. Such a colony as they would plant on the Ohio was precisely what the sagacious among public men had long sought.

Thus far the West was in the most unsatisfactory condition—a menace to the Union rather than an assurance of safety. Washington had not long before this said: "The Western States stand, as it were, upon a pivot—the touch of a feather would turn them any way"—and he had advised the applying of "the cement of interest to bind all parts of the Union together by indissoluble bonds." The fact that the character of the men proposing to plant a colony on the Ohio was beyond question, and that their ability and disposition gave double guarantee that they would bind the West to the East "by indissoluble bonds," constituted the inducement that moved Congress almost unanimously and

Ohio and Her Western Reserve

with startling celerity to pass the ordinance. Thus a mere handful of intending settlers of Ohio dictated and secured the fundamental law for the whole Northwest Territory, and made it free soil forever. Seldom in all history has so momentous a result proceeded from so relatively an insignificant cause.

The next year—on April 7, 1788—the pioneer contingent of the New England Ohio Company—led by General Rufus Putnam, of Massachusetts, a distinguished officer of the Revolution, and nephew of General Israel Putnam—dropping down the "beautiful river" from Pittsburg in a rude boat, appropriately named the Mayflower, landed at the mouth of the Muskingum and founded Marietta, the first organized, lawful English settlement in a State which, so far from ever

Gen. RUFUS PUTNAM.

CAMPUS MARTIUS.
First home of the first settlers of Ohio, at Marietta.

The "Great Ordinance" of 1787

being open to the imputation of standing "upon a pivot," was speedily to become and forever remain one of the firmest buttresses of the Federal Union.

There had been prior to this time a straggling and sparse fringe of frontiersmen along the west bank of the Ohio, people who occupied the backwoods very much as did the pioneers of Kentucky; but there was no organized settlement, and no legal settlement, because until the time of the Ohio Company's purchase there had been no law laid upon the land. Christian Frederick Post, the Moravian missionary, had in 1761 built a cabin on the Tuscarawas, which it is supposed was the first white man's house in the limits of the future Ohio; and in 1785-'86 the government had built, at the mouth of the Muskingum, Fort Harmar, where a small garrison was maintained. This, though not a settlement, served admirably to protect that made at Marietta on the opposite shore.

Thus to all intents and purposes the beginnings of Ohio were made, as has been related, by the New Englanders at Marietta. They began the progressive and permanent occupation of the region that was to become

Ohio and Her Western Reserve

Ohio, and were the true pioneers of civilization within its limits. They immediately set up the institutions of local government, opened schools and a church, and prudentially enclosed their homes in a fort which they called "Campus Martius," and which afforded them a sense of security during the period of Indian hostilities—mostly far away. It was from these soldier settlers of Marietta, and in the very first days of their Ohio residence, that there came the favorite and famous nickname of the State. They were greatly admired by the Indians because of their generally high stature and erect and soldierly bearing, and one of them who was particularly the object of adulation, Colonel Ebenezer Sproat, who stood six feet four and as straight as the Indians themselves, they called "Hetuck"—that is, the Buckeye—which in Ohio, at least, was a tree conspicuous for its height and symmetry. Gradually the name became a generic appellation for the early Ohioans, and finally, in the "log-cabin campaign" of 1840, was firmly fixed upon the State.

The enactment of the great ordinance had set others than the New Englanders upon the

The "Great Ordinance" of 1787

project of casting their fortunes in the West, and several movements were quickly made tending toward that end. John Cleves Symmes and associates, of New Jersey, in the same year purchased a million acres of land on the Ohio between the two Miami Rivers, and, spurred to emulation by the *éclat* with which the wild had been opened at Marietta, these people made three settlements within their tract before the expiration of 1788, the second of which, founded December 24th, as Losantiville, became famous as Cincinnati, for nearly a century the metropolis of Ohio, and justly entitled the "Queen City of the West."

JOHN CLEVES SYMMES.

In the meantime, on July 15, 1788, was formally instituted at Marietta the first government, save in a mere nominal sense, that had ever held sway over the vast Northwest Territory. Congress had on October 5, 1787,

Ohio and Her Western Reserve

elected its president, General Arthur St. Clair, as Governor of the Territory, but he had only now arrived in the settlement. Winthrop Sargent had been made secretary, Samuel Holden Parsons, James M. Varnum, and John Cleves Symmes judges. In their various nativities these men gave some suggestion of the composite nature of the population which was destined to characterize Ohio, to constitute one of its chief claims to uniqueness, and to figure as a leading source of its ultimate strength. St. Clair was a Scotchman, in America since the French and Indian War, and at the time of his appointment a Pennsylvanian. Sargent was from Massachusetts, Parsons from Connecticut, Varnum from Rhode Island, and Symmes from New Jersey.

The Territorial period abounded with occurrences of important nature, only two or three of which, however, will be mentioned here, as either necessary to show the sequence of events or having a bearing upon the future of the State, among other causes, which it is purposed to set forth. Of the latter class, of what may be called causative happenings, were the Indian wars, of which the chief

The "Great Ordinance" of 1787

events were St. Clair's defeat and Wayne's victory. These were events in themselves of large importance, if we recall that the casualties in the former were far larger, and the results of the latter, greater than in any battle of the Revolution. But they were far more significant to the people of the West, in that they afforded a palpable demonstration that the Federal army was fighting for their benefit, and because of that reflection laying in the breasts of the frontiersmen a feeling of gratitude, and rendering deeper that dignifying sense of nationalism which had its beginning in the understanding of the principles of the great ordinance and the peculiar conditions of the cosmopolitan settlement of the country.

The Territorial government had for sometime little to do in a civil way, for the great influx of people had not yet set in, and it was estimated that in 1790 the whole vast Territory had a population of only about 4,300 souls, of whom nearly one-half were in the remote French settlements of Kaskaskia, Vincennes, and Sault Ste. Marie.

But the year 1796 marked the beginning

Ohio and Her Western Reserve

of big accessions, and was one of the most important in the history of the State It was then that, Wayne's victory and treaty having dispelled all apprehension of Indian hostility, settlers came more numerously into that part of the Territory that in less than a decade was to be carved into Ohio. And it was then that the remarkable compositeness of population heretofore alluded to was to be carried a few steps farther in its inclusion of variety. Its settlements formerly consisted mainly of Massachusetts men (at Marietta) and of New Jersey men (in and about Cincinnati); but now were thrown open to incomers the huge tracts reserved respectively by Virginia and Connecticut, the former including more than 4,000,000 acres, known as the Virginia Military District, shaped like a wedge, with its broad base resting on the Ohio, and its point extending northward between the Scioto and Miami Rivers, to the very heart of the State; and the latter consisting of nearly 3,000,000 acres extending in an oblong, 120 miles from the boundary of Pennsylvania along Lake Erie. The first of these, reserved by Virginia for the rewards of its Revolution-

The "Great Ordinance" of 1787

ary soldiers, was settled this year at Chillicothe by a company from Kentucky (although they were originally Virginians) led by General Nathaniel Massie; and the Connecticut Reserve, held by the Yankee State for the benefit of her school fund, was settled by a little band of her own colonists led by General Moses Cleaveland, who left his name upon the geography of Ohio, in the town which he founded, now become the chief city of the State. In the meantime the Symmes settlements had been extended to Dayton, and the lands lying across the Ohio west of Pennsylvania and Virginia—and between the Ohio Company's purchase on the South and the Connecticut Reserve on the North, which had been surveyed as the "Seven Ranges," the first of all the Congress lands in the whole public domain—were receiving their share of immigration, mainly from the contiguous territory across the river. And so it came about that by the year 1796 the future State had five separate bodies of population, and of as many distinct elements or origins.

Of all of these, the Virginia element, which had, from the first, men of marked

Ohio and Her Western Reserve

ability in its midst, more attracted others, and partly because of the bestowal of land upon its Revolutionary officers, and partly because these lands were of an excellence which made them desirable to settlers, who readily purchased them, grew most rapidly, and by the time Ohio came to be ushered into organic being as a State, dominated not only its founding, but for a considerable period its destinies. Chillicothe, as a daughter of Virginia, with a certain poetical propriety, became the mother of governors and the nourisher of robust politicians.

These Virginians formed the nucleus of the new Western Democracy, and rallying around them the sympathizers with their faith to be found scattered here and there through the other settlements, taking advantage of the rise of the Jeffersonian Republican party in national affairs and the political exigencies of its leader, which would be well served by the creation of a new State—taking advantage, too, of that spirit of advanced and pronounced democratic feeling always evident on the frontier, and more than all else, of the increasing personal unpopularity of Governor

The "Great Ordinance" of 1787

St. Clair—they overruled the opposing Federalists who had their strongholds in the less populous settlements of the Ohio Company and in the Western Reserve, and created the State of Ohio. The Massachusetts and New England Federalists of Marietta before their feet touched the soil had given the region that they were to make their home a marvelous and far-reaching fundamental law, providing for the exclusion of slavery forever and the "support of religion and learning," but it remained for the Virginians (with a small sprinkling from some of the other elements of the composite population) to give the territory statehood.

CHAPTER IX

OHIO ACHIEVES STATEHOOD

If Ohio has experienced a prominence more conspicuous in the field of politics than in any other, it has come naturally by that peculiar form of prestige, for it was born, so to speak, at the close of one of the most adroit and intricate political schemings, and in one of the fiercest of political fights, and if the State has been determinedly devoted to politics, its choice may be very appropriately ascribed to the mysterious influence of prenatal impression.

Statehood was not achieved by a stroke. Even its immediate causes commenced their operation fully five years before the consummation was reached. They were complicated; and it is difficult to follow the chief ones through the tangled skein, but a little time may, perhaps, be profitably taken for unravel-

Ohio Achieves Statehood

ing the inveterately involved strands of causation which led a century ago to the creation of one of the greatest of the United States.

Of the first, we have already seen something in the circumstantially favored development of the democratic settlements at Chillicothe. This was the more significant as it came coincidentally with the rise of the Republican and Democratic power in the nation, at the beginning of the century. The central location of this settlement was a powerful factor in the whole movement, as it led to its aspiration to become a capital—first of the Territory, and then of a permanent government—and so organized and energized the political powers of its people.

A subsequent contributory cause was to be found in the advance of the Territory to its second phase—involving an elective Assembly in addition to the Governor's Council—to which it became entitled in 1798, by the number of its male inhabitants reaching 5,000. This and the close following reduction of its territory by the erection of Indiana Territory, (which left the old Northwest Territory including little besides the present State of

Ohio and Her Western Reserve

Ohio, plus half the lower peninsula of Michigan, embracing Detroit), were momentous moves potently influencing the ascendency of the Democracy, the downfall of Federalism, and the creation of Ohio as a State.

The earliest of these measures had brought prominently to the front in civil life the first of the "Ohio Presidents," William Henry Harrison, already famed in war, having served at Fallen Timbers as Wayne's aide, and destined to be the hero of Tippecanoe. He was chosen as the first Territorial Delegate to Congress and rendered valuable service, especially in land legislation. On the erection of Indiana Territory in 1800, he was made its Governor, and his popular fulfilment of the duties of that position made St. Clair, who was still Governor of the diminished Northwest Territory, suffer from comparison. But the diminution of the original territory had already hurt St. Clair sufficiently to insure his political demise. It was a Republican measure and designed to accomplish, among other things, that end.

Animosity toward Arthur St. Clair undoubtedly hastened the creation of the State.

Ohio Achieves Statehood

It seems pitiful that the degradation of this doubly unfortunate, but pure and lofty man, should have been inseparably associated with the rise of a great State, but such was the case. And St. Clair was not only ignominiously beaten and deposed from his high position, but the progress of the whole propaganda resulting in his defeat and the triumphant bourgeoning of Ohio was accompanied by bitterness of spirit and vituperativeness of utterance, reaching a climax in riotous demonstrations and threats of violence and death.

The whole trouble arose from the fact that as Governor of the Territory St. Clair had rather large powers, and he was so constituted as not only to make the most of them, but to enlarge upon his prerogatives in a manner that was military and foreign rather than civil and in accordance with the new Americanism which now more than ever, and in the West more than elsewhere, was trending away from aristocracy and autocracy and toward democracy. He was especially charged with a frequent autocratic and tyrannical exercise of the veto power. St. Clair was by birth a Scotchman and by education a soldier.

Ohio and Her Western Reserve

He was a Federalist, but it defines him better to say that he was an aristocrat rather than a democrat. Unlike Harrison, he was utterly out of touch with the Western character. He had ability, but no adaptability, and contact with the rough and ready men of the frontier democracy whom he distrusted and sought to govern autocratically only developed keener irritation and deeper dislike upon both sides. He was intensely loyal to the party which had placed him in office and to his old commander, Washington, and there exists not the slightest ground for doubt that he believed that he only did his duty and labored for what he sincerely regarded as the best interests of the country, but he went down under a storm of obloquy, in a large measure undeserved, and he merited far better treatment than he received—alike from the pioneer

Ohio Achieves Statehood

Ohioans, the people of the country, and the Government. When he died, in poverty and obscurity, at his retreat near Ligonier, Pa., in 1818, it could be said that the man who first administered the laws of the United States in the most important Territory it ever organized was an honest man and a gentleman to the last.

At the time of the advancement of the Territory to its second form of government St. Clair and his Federalist upholders—the chief of whom were Jacob Burnet of the Cincinnati settlement, and the Marietta men—had sought to have the eastern territory consist only of the lands between the Ohio on the east and the Scioto on the west, which would have completely eliminated Chillicothe, and established a territory half the size of Ohio, which could have no hope of statehood for many years, and would pretty surely remain under St. Clair's dominion.

In 1801 they still stood by these lines on which their opponents had once defeated them. But the creation of a State rather than a Territory had now become the issue. Whether they were altogether sincere or not

Ohio and Her Western Reserve

is now impossible to determine, but at all events the Federalists, who had then a majority in the Territorial legislature, in November, 1801, passed a bill for the erection of a State on the lines they had formerly proposed for a Territory—that is, making the eastern boundary of the State those of Pennsylvania and Virginia along the Ohio, and the western one the Scioto, and a line drawn from its intersection with the Indian boundary line, northeastwardly, to the west corner of the Connecticut Reserve. It is needless to say that had this scheme succeeded Ohio would never have become "one of the principal divisions of the earth," nor would it have achieved the particular prominence which has characterized it, for it would have been less than one-half its present size.

St. Clair and his followers in urging these narrow limits possibly thought they would create a State which they could control; but more probably their aim was to project one that would fail of creation, thereby prolonging the existence of the Territorial government until a period possibly more propitious for a change in their own interests. The narrow

Ohio Achieves Statehood

limits which they prescribed were not altogether within the spirit of the provisions of the Ordinance of 1787, which declared for the creation of from three to five States from the Territory; but, on the other hand, they did not represent an absolute innovation of idea, for Timothy Pickering and Thomas Jefferson had early favored a plan of subdivision which would have carved the Northwest Territory into ten, instead of the present five States. Jefferson just at this juncture, however, had a desire for a very different kind of State than the little one which St. Clair and the Federalists proposed presenting to the Union, and he was destined to have it in due season, but not entirely without difficulty.

Right on the heels of the bill for their little Federalist State the followers of St. Clair rather injudiciously put through another for the removal of the Territorial capital from Chillicothe to Cincinnati. To be left out of the future State and to lose in the present the capital was altogether too much for the Virginia democracy of Chillicothe to endure passively. They resented it, and the full fury of their resentment fell suddenly.

Ohio and Her Western Reserve

They held St. Clair chiefly responsible for both measures, and his attempted tampering with the Territorial lines had previously aroused their enmity. It had long smoldered, but this fresh assault upon their interests, capped by the capital removal, fanned their anger into flaming outburst which wellnigh proved fatal to the hated Governor.

A mob rioted through the streets of the frontier capital on the night after the passage of the last of the offensive measures, and under the leadership of one Michael Baldwin, a brilliant but turbulent character, whose counterpart has existed in every Western settlement, sought to force its way into St. Clair's lodgings, presumably to drag him forth and inflict violence upon his offensively august person. But St. Clair was saved from such indignity and danger by the better element of his own bitterest opponents, Thomas Worthington—a future Ohio Governor—and others. That these men did not lose their heads during the whirlwind of passion, was testified to by the Governor himself, who put himself on record by allusion to the "splendid exertion" of Mr. Worthington, "who was

Ohio Achieves Statehood

obliged to go so far as to threaten him [Baldwin] with death."

This, of course, was the action merely of the lower class of the enraged partizans—the class which usually acts first and thinks afterward. But the better class were not much slower of action, for a crisis had arisen, and with a foresight that was creditable to them, the Republican-Democrats saw that the ship of State might be launched and they left ashore! They not only wanted to be aboard the good ship Ohio, but to have a hand in fashioning her and setting her sails and serving at the wheel. So Thomas Worthington went on to the national capital to see what could be done there. That the riotous Michael, surnamed Baldwin, was regarded in the light of something more than a mere brawler and mob leader, we shall see again, but for the present it was sufficient demonstration of his worth that Worthington took him with him to Washington. Possibly he was afraid to leave him at home during his absence, for fear he might fall upon the Governor.

The potential Ohio was now projected

Ohio and Her Western Reserve

into national politics, already a seething and hissing caldron.

Jefferson had been admonished by the narrow margin of his election over Burr that a few more electoral votes to look to in the future would be a comfortable thing, and that the party might actually need them for a continuance in power. The Western Republican-Democrats in all of their efforts toward the creation of a State planned primarily for one that should be Democratic. That would mean three more presidential electors and two more Senators. Success on the side of the Federalists meant just as much to them. Neither cared a whit for a State unless it could be the kind of State they should dictate. Each ached for it with an intense passion if it could be made to their own desire. In the end it proved that the Federalists only aspired—though they continued to ache—and the Democrats achieved and enjoyed. Viewed nationally, the new State might make or unmake a President and decide the balance of the great parties and policies; and thus in the meantime Ohio was a hugely important political makeweight even before it had

Ohio Achieves Statehood

issued from the limbo of the problematic into the arena of the actual.

Thomas Worthington, the able and active Jeffersonian, to whom more than to any other one man the final establishment of Ohio was due, soon found that the temper of Congress was such as not only to repudiate the Federalist movement for a feeble State (excluding one-half of the present Ohio), but that the body would go further and consider the claims for statehood of the larger Territory that the Republicans favored. Paul Fearing presented the Federalist legislative enactment to Congress on January 20, 1802, and the opposition to it on the part of the Jeffersonians immediately began to be vigorously made manifest. While Worthington labored in Washington his adherents carried on a tumultuous campaign in the Territory, and forwarded formidable petitions to

THOMAS WORTHINGTON.

Ohio and Her Western Reserve

Congress in support of their greater State proposition.

The battle in the Territory was complicated and given an additional heat by the fervid opposition to St. Clair, who sought statehood fully as much for his elimination from their political life as they did for the benefits of the measure itself. In fact, most of their invective was directed against him. They called him and his adherents "Tories" and declared the Territorial government an oppressive one, and St. Clair, whom they dubbed "Arthur the First," a "tyrant who must be curbed." The country was filled with a clamor "to shake off the iron fetters of aristocracy" and bring about "the downfall of the Tory party in the Territory," while the mild measures which had been resorted to to induce President Adams not to reappoint St. Clair were succeeded by more vigorous ones seeking his dismissal from office by the newly elected Republican President. The latter action, as we shall see, was an extreme from which Jefferson held himself aloof until St. Clair, who was evidently goaded to desperation by the inevitableness

Ohio Achieves Statehood

of his downfall, himself precipitated it by intemperate utterance.

The upshot of all this war in the West by the Republicans and labor in Congress by Worthington was that the act of the Federalist Legislature was rejected in the House by a vote of 81 to 5, which showed conclusively how offensive it was. The Rev. Manasseh Cutler, who had been instrumental in framing the Ordinance of 1787, was now a member of Congress and one of the five who voted for the limited State in violation, as to boundaries, of the very ordinance he had secured the passage of. But he was a pronounced Federalist.

The Jeffersonians followed up this victory to secure its fruits, and under the lead of Breckenridge in the Senate and Giles in the House passed a bill which became a law April 30, 1802, by the President's approval, known as the "Enabling Act," the first of its kind in our legislation and the model for many in the future, paving the way for the admission of Ohio to the Union, and constituted precisely as it now is, save for a slight difference in the Michigan boundary.

Ohio and Her Western Reserve

It is significant of the attitude of the Southern and Middle States toward the West at this time, that of 47 votes cast for the admission of Ohio into the Union 26 came from the South, 14 from the Middle States, and only 9 from New England. Virginia voted solidly for the measure; Massachusetts' vote was equally divided; Connecticut was 0 for and 5 against the establishment of the State.

Thus in a few months the tables were completely turned against the Federalists, and the Republicans were well advanced toward final victory. It only remained for the people to clinch what had been gained.

The "Enabling Act" had authorized a convention of delegates from all that part of the Territory proposed for statehood—all except Wayne County, including the eastern half of the lower peninsula of Michigan—to be held November 1st, at Chillicothe, to determine if it was expedient to establish a State government, and, if so, to proceed to frame a constitution and form a government, or to call another convention for that purpose. A hotly contested campaign for

Ohio Achieves Statehood

the election of delegates ensued, the issue being State or no State. There were multitudinous objections on the part of the Federalists, and all of the old charges against St. Clair were made to do duty again by the Jeffersonians, as well as new arguments setting forth the benefits to be derived from a State government. The strongest contention of the Federalists was that the Territory had not yet the 60,000 population required by the ordinance to entitle it to statehood; but this had little effect, and only proved their own insincerity in moving, as they had done, for a State of far smaller bounds. It was true that a census taken in January, 1802, showed but 45,028 people of both sexes and all ages in the Territory, but the Republicans argued that the population would reach the required figure by the time that statehood was achieved, and it was obvious enough that a State which included the Chillicothe and Cincinnati settlements would sooner reach the required population than one which did not. One of the ludicrous objections of the Federalists, which, of course, seems even smaller now than it did when made, was that the Terri-

Ohio and Her Western Reserve

torial government only cost about $5,000 per year, and that the expenses of a State government would be fully $15,000! But the opposition soon weakened.

When the convention assembled it was overwhelmingly Republican. It not only quickly decided the question of statehood for Ohio, but that it would itself prescribe the constitution for the State instead of leaving that task to a second convention, and went ahead with the work so expeditiously that it adjourned on the 29th of the month, having completed its duties.

What might be called the last protest of the Federalists was also the final gasp of its leader, poor Arthur St. Clair. He asked permission to address the convention, and although fourteen members voted against his doing so, he made a most injudicious speech, in which he inveighed against the "Enabling Act" as "an interference by Congress in the internal affairs of the country, such as they had neither the power nor right to make, not binding on the people and in truth a nullity," with much of contempt, and when this had been promptly conveyed to President Jeffer-

Ohio Achieves Statehood

son, there soon came like a thunderbolt to the old Governor a curt communication from Secretary of State James Madison (acting under orders from President Jefferson) alluding to his "intemperance and indecorum of language toward the Legislature of the United States," his "disorganizing spirit and tendency of very evil example," and peremptorily dismissing him from his high office. Thus after fourteen years of service General Arthur St. Clair was cut short in his incumbency in an office which was itself to end in a few months, and the letter containing his dismissal was handed him by his secretary and bitter enemy, now made his successor. But there was little sympathy for St. Clair among the triumphant Republicans in convention assembled and about to launch Ohio.

Another episode of the convention, peculiar and significant of the fact that the battle for free soil in Ohio and the old Northwest was not wholly nor immediately won by the ordinance of freedom, consisted in the actual attempt made to introduce, constitutionally, a limited slavery. The integrity of the ordinance was first attacked in Ohio, as it was

Ohio and Her Western Reserve

afterward and more persistently in the other two Ohio River States of the Territory. An effort was made in the Committee that framed the Bill of Rights of the Constitution to introduce a clause favoring a form of slavery in which male slaves might be held until thirty-five years of age and females until twenty-eight years old, and it was alleged by the delegate offering this provision that one of the greatest men of the nation (it was believed the allusion was to Jefferson) thought that "this would be a great step toward a general emancipation of slavery" in the whole country. But there was upon this committee, as a Federalist delegate from the Marietta district, Ephraim Cutler, a son of Dr. Manasseh Cutler, credited with the antislavery provision of the ordinance, and he made radical objection to slavery being allowed a foothold in the State, framed a clause of the constitution in the very language of the ordinance, and, rising from a sick bed, fought it to adoption, though it was saved both in committee and convention by a majority of only one. On this action rests Judge Cutler's title to the gratitude of the people of the

Ohio Achieves Statehood

Northwest, a title exceeded by that of no other man, and only equaled perhaps by the splendid service of Edward Coles, of Illinois (who was, by the way, of Southern birth). The stand taken by Cutler in reaffirming the sixth compact of the ordinance exerted an influence early and late, repeatedly, as other States and Territories sought, in the interests of Southern immigration, to evade it. Not a twelvemonth had elapsed when the people of Indiana Territory urging Congress to set aside this article, John Randolph answered them nay and held up Ohio as an example of what a State might become without the aid of slavery.

The constitution adopted at Chillicothe was the work of many hands. It is traditionally asserted that the same swashbuckling but brilliant Michael Baldwin whom we have seen leading the mob against St. Clair was its principal author, and that he used a whisky barrel as a desk on which to write it, and some of the contents as the spirit of literary inspiration. But there is a preponderance of probability amounting almost to a certainty that the real author of the instru-

Ohio and Her Western Reserve

ment was Judge Jacob Burnet, of Cincinnati, a native of Newark, N. J., born 1770, a graduate of Princeton, the leading lawyer of the State, and "the Lycurgus of the West." Originally a Federalist, and later a Whig, he was successively Supreme Court Judge and United States Senator, and no man made a deeper impression upon the history of Ohio.

Judge JACOB BURNET.

The present President of the United States has called it a "foolish" constitution, but it was wise in one provision — viz., against the possible contingency of any Governor becoming too strenuous in the exercise of an unpopular policy. It went to the democratic extremity of limiting the Governor's powers to almost nil, and conferring all the patronage on the Legislature.

When "Tom" Corwin was Governor he remarked, after a week's occupation of the office, that "reprieving criminals and appoint-

Ohio Achieves Statehood

ing notaries were the sole powers of the prerogative." The truth was that the shadow of St. Clair fell athwart the making of the Ohio constitution and influenced the limitation of the executive power. Even after the lapse of half a century, when Ohio, having in the meantime thrived very well under the original, made a new constitution, the memory of the stiff old autocrat was still a restraining force, and the State to this day is one of the four in the whole Union in which the Governor has no veto.

Ohio was never formally admitted, as all other States since the original thirteen have been, to the Union; and it has been a matter of much contention as to which one of half a dozen dates is the true one from which to compute her age. That of April 30, 1802, is not the correct one. It is simply that of the passage of the " Enabling Act." A better one would be that of November 29th, in the same year, when the constitution was adopted, or January 11, 1803, when the first election was held; but these and several others are unsupportable for various reasons. On February 19, 1803, Congress passed an act "for the

Ohio and Her Western Reserve

execution of the laws of the United States within the State of Ohio," and this was the nearest approach to the "act of admission," from which the existence of the other States is dated. This date has been generally sanctioned by the historians as the true one. But the Legislature first assembled on March 1, 1803, and the Ohio Archeological and Historical Society has officially decided that date to be the proper one of the State's origin, and it is therefore now generally so accepted.

The new ultrademocratic State, which had been protesting against the survival of English methods in its colonial government, elected as its first Governor British-born Edward Tiffin, who had presided over the constitutional convention, and with the exception

EDWARD TIFFIN.

Ohio Achieves Statehood

that one place on the Supreme Court judiciary was given to a Federalist — Samuel Huntington, of the Connecticut Reserve — the spoils of office naturally went to the Jeffersonians, who held dominion over their own creation for more than twenty years. Thomas Worthington received substantial reward for his great services as a State founder in being made one of its first United States Senators, his colleague being John Smith; and Jeremiah Morrow was elected and remained for ten years the sole Representative in Congress.

Of all the measures accompanying the advance to statehood, by far the most important, because powerfully affecting the settlement, and consequently the rapid rise of the State in every way, was a clause inserted by Albert Gallatin in the "Enabling Act" of Congress (and having all the force of a contract, when accepted, as it was, by the people of the State), which provided that the United States should grant one-twentieth of the proceeds of all lands sold in the State to the construction of roads connecting tide-water with the Western waters. This was the real

Ohio and Her Western Reserve

beginning of internal improvements in this country, and resulted in the building of the famous National Road to and through Ohio, a work costing several millions, and fully as important in its time as the construction of the transcontinental railroad in a later and larger era. The Ohioans were never in danger of becoming "separatists," like the people of their Southern neighbors—as was indicated by Burr's finding them "too plodding for his purpose"; but Gallatin's far foreseeing cemented them even more firmly to the Union, and the inauguration of the policy of public improvements put the settlements of Ohio fully twenty years ahead.

CHAPTER X

OHIO'S ASCENDENCY ANALYZED

THE remarkably rapid progress of Ohio's settlement constitutes one of the most wonderful chapters in the history of the nation, and taken together with·the cosmopolitanism that characterized it, gives to the State its best title to be considered, at least in one respect, absolutely unique among the sisterhood of States, as has already been claimed in a preceding chapter. That the distinction is true, and not a mere figure of speech, becomes apparent upon even a slight examination of the facts.

Cutler's construction and passage of the Ordinance of 1787 have been dwelt on as constituting *the first great humanly planned* cause of Ohio's early auspiciousness of condition. Taken in conjunction with the *first great fortuitous cause of rapid settlement,* her

Ohio and Her Western Reserve

geographical position, these two were sufficient to work seeming wonders, but Gallatin's stroke of economic statesmanship came as a third great formative cause, supplementing and enormously enhancing the effect of the others. Geographically, Ohio stood, a great body of desirable, nationalized land, as the focusing-point of a cordon of settled States, naturally looked to by all as a field of settlement. Then came the ordinance operating automatically for selection of the best from these. And finally Gallatin's great provision for preparing a highway for the march of civilization. It was all exactly as if the concentrating march of a vast army of occupation had been directed upon Ohio as a huge strategic movement planned by a supreme commander of sublime intelligence and foreseeingly carried forward as a single gigantic operation—engineering measures and all—from the first to the finish. But if the result of several statesmen's sagacity, all building wiser than they knew, and singularly favored by the fortuitous, the end was the same.

It has been tritely told that New England was sown with selected seed from Old Eng-

Ohio's Ascendency Analyzed

land. But Ohio was sown with selected seed from New England and all the colonies. Her uniqueness, historically speaking, lies in the fact that hers was the first soil settled by the United States.

New England was peopled by the Puritans (and others) from old England; New York, by Dutch and English; Pennsylvania, by Quakers and Germans and Scotch-Irish; Virginia, again by English, but quite different from those of Massachusetts and Connecticut; Maryland, by still another element; and so on. Of the States not included among the original thirteen, but admitted to the Union before Ohio, Vermont was settled by Massachusetts and New York, Kentucky by Virginia, and Tennessee by North Carolina; but Ohio was settled by all of these—by elements from each and every State in the confederacy; in other words, Ohio was settled by the people of the United States.

Hers was the first territory to be representative of the entire people. Within her borders the hitherto racially different or long-separated consanguineous elements—in some instances estranged, in others emasculated or

Ohio and Her Western Reserve

enervated through dearth of fresh blood—came into contiguity—finally to be blent into a homogeneous whole, and so to advance by another stage—and a huge one—the evolution of a race. It would savor of extremism to go further and to say that these once widely dissevered and dissimilar elements coming together in a virgin land not only advanced an old, but founded a new race; and yet, what were those elementary fragments in the old States but colonies of English Puritans and Cavaliers and Quakers, of Scotch-Irish and Germans? And, in a certain sense, were not the Ohioans truly the first Americans?

A slight analysis of this surprisingly varied population is interesting, both because of the reminders it affords of the origins of some prominent Ohio personages, and its revelation of the influence of the old States in building a new one.

No two or three States can be credited with a preponderating contribution to Ohio if its whole history is taken into account, but because of its territory lying in the zone of Virginia's and Pennsylvania's natural emigra-

Ohio's Ascendency Analyzed

tion westward, and because these States were nearest and most populous, it was their pioneers who dominated the new State during the years that it was new. This fact is attested by the prevalence of men born in those two States, among the constitution makers and early Congressmen of Ohio. Of twelve men in the convention of 1802 whose history is known, six came from Virginia, one each from Pennsylvania, Maryland, North Carolina, and Connecticut, and two from Massachusetts. Of Congressmen prior to 1830, out of thirty-three whose nativity is known, nine were Pennsylvanians, six Virginians, six also each from Connecticut and New Jersey, three from New York, and one each from Massachusetts, New Hampshire, and Kentucky.

Virginia gave the State the first of its presidential contributions—William Henry Harrison. It gave it, too, its chief of founders, Thomas Worthington, later Senator and Governor, and those other sterling early Governors, Allen Trimble and Robert Lucas; its eminent jurist, Noah H. Swayne, Justice of the Supreme Court of the United States; its

Ohio and Her Western Reserve

pioneer and founder of the State capital, Lucas Sullivant and Lyne Starling; its famous Ewing family and Allen G. Thurman—with many more almost equally influential men.

Pennsylvania in the early days was not far behind Virginia as an Ohio builder. She

sent over her western border General William Lytle, the founder of an influential Ohio family, of whom the poet-soldier, General William H. Lytle, was a representative of the third generation; Joseph Vance, twice a strong member of Congress and twice Governor; Jeremiah Morrow, sole member of Congress from Ohio, 1803 to 1813, and last of the pioneer Governors; that strangely named Quaker abolitionist, Achilles Pugh; General Thomas Lyon Hamer, the only rival of Corwin, martyr hero of the Mexican War, and the Congressman who sent Grant to West Point; John A. Bingham, Congress-

Ohio's Ascendency Analyzed

man and foreign minister, and variously prominent in the nation; the father of General William S. Rosecrans; "the fighting McCooks'" progenitors; the nearest ancestry of General Grant; and the parents of the late President McKinley.

New Jersey, smaller and more remote, did less, but still much. What she did is suggested, rather than told, in the names of her pioneers, among whom, besides John Cleves Symmes, the founder of Cincinnati, were Jacob Burnet, "the Lycurgus of the West"; the Zanes, highest types of the frontiersmen; Benjamin Lundy, the journalistic pioneer of antislavery agitation in State and nation; John McLean, of the United States Supreme Court, who dared to dissent from Taney on the Dred Scott decision; the Piatts, of poetic fame; Nicholas Longworth, philanthropist and munificent patron of art; and the father of Wil-

Ohio and Her Western Reserve

liam Dennison, one of the triumvirate of the State's great "war Governors."

Kentucky contributed the peerless "Tom" Corwin, Governor and Senator of the United States, equally famous as sound statesman and brilliant wit; General Irvin McDowell, and—strangely exemplifying the automatic working of the great ordinance—James G. Birney, pioneer of abolition.

Maryland sent to the State, as the most prominent of her pioneers, Charles S. Hammond, the great editor and lawyer, and as the most prominent of later-day citizens, Hugh J. Jewett, financier.

From North Carolina, though far away, came many who achieved eminence themselves or were the parents of eminent men. Among the former, the ancestors of Edwin M. Stanton, the iron War Secretary, and of Murat Halstead, and among the latter Wil-

Ohio's Ascendency Analyzed

liam Allen, Congressman and most famous of Ohio's Democratic Governors; also—again illustrating the function of selection in the ordinance—Levi Coffin, most prominent of emancipators, who freed from two to three thousand slaves by personal exertions, and passed into history as the "reputed president of the Underground Railroad."

New England, aside from the Marietta settlement, composed principally of Massachusetts men, and including the Putnams and Cutlers, whose great services to the State have been shown, and Return Jonathan Meigs, an early Governor and Ohio's first of a long series of contributions to the Cabinets,—did not figure so largely in the early weaving of the Western social fabric as did the Middle and Southern States. But New England made up for this omission when the Connecticut Reserve was opened to settle-

Ohio and Her Western Reserve

ment. Connecticut men naturally predominated there, as we have already seen. Samuel Huntington, one of the first judges of the Ohio Supreme Court and second Governor of the State, was of the vanguard of her pioneers. Here also came from the same Yankee State the father of David Tod, second of the "war Governors." But Connecticut's contribution was not all bestowed on her Reserve. Alfred Kelley, of Columbus, "the father of the Ohio canal system," was of Connecticut derivation, as was the late Governor George Hoadley, of Cincinnati, and so also Morrison R. Waite, of Toledo, Chief Justice of the United States, and the Sherman family of the central part of the State, whose name was made illustrious by the longest-serving Senator of the United States and its most famous financier, John Sherman, and by General William Tecumseh Sherman.

To Massachusetts must be accredited "Ben" Wade and Joshua R. Giddings, the twin political giants of the Reserve (although the latter was born, where the family a short time sojourned, in Pennsylvania). Garfield,

Ohio's Ascendency Analyzed

of the same region, also came remotely of mingled Massachusetts and Connecticut stock.

Vermont "Green Mountain" vigor was exhibited in a goodly immigration, which bore in, among others, Governor Reuben Wood, and the father of President Rutherford B. Hayes, of Fremont. Rhode Island would have been well enough represented even had she sent to the new State no other of her sons than the lofty Whig leader, Samuel F. Vinton. New Hampshire contributed Lewis Cass, whom Ohio lost to Michigan's gain, and Salmon P. Chase, Lincoln's Secretary of the Treasury and Chief Justice of the United States.

New York added to this composite population, among a host of useful and famous citizens, General Duncan McArthur, one of the pioneer Governors; the great jurist, Joseph R. Swan; Attorney-General Henry Stanberry;

Ohio and Her Western Reserve

Major-General Jacob D. Cox; Eleutheros Cooke, the father of Jay Cooke; also the fathers of General McPherson and James A. Garfield.

If we go further and consider nationalities, we find that these added to the complexity of population and contributed elements of power. Of the Germans, it is sufficient to say, look at Cincinnati, with its musical and art fame! But of this people there came even the despised Hessians, and behold the son of one of them was the brave cavalryman Custer! If we turn to the English of immediate immigration, we are reminded that of these were Tiffin, the first Governor of the State, and John Brough, the greatest of its war Governors. From the British isle of Guernsey, on the French coast, came enough people to decide the naming of a county after their native island. Even the French, who were a small element, brought some fine strains of blood, of which one comes down to to-day in the literary elegance of Mrs. Madeline Vinton Dahlgren. The pure Dutch gave the State the able Brinkerhoffs, and the nation, through the State, one of its greatest

Ohio's Ascendency Analyzed

generals, William S. Rosecrans, whose fame grows brighter with the passing years. The Scotch-Irish, always strong in the frontier settlements, contributed the Covenanter stock of which Whitelaw Reid came; that of Governor Joseph Vance; of Generals McDowell, McPherson, and Steedman; that of the "fighting McCooks," fifteen in number, all famous; and the blood on his father's side of U. S. Grant. As for the straight Irish, they here lost no time in showing their proneness to politics and fighting. First of them all was Michael Baldwin, whom we have seen rioting at Chillicothe in the period of the State's formation, and who was also the first Speaker of the Ohio House. Wilson Shannon, the first native-born Governor, was an Irishman; and so, too, General Phil Sheridan, and the brilliant war correspondent Januarius Aloysius MacGahan, the "Bulgarian liberator."

The exceedingly diversified elements of population which have been indicated underwent the first great step toward homogeneity in the stirring times of the War of 1812. The intensely patriotic and energetic spirit of the pioneers was splendidly attested when a popu-

Ohio and Her Western Reserve

lation which cast a total vote of about 19,000 contributed over 20,000 men to the military service. Here occurred the first demonstration of Ohio's usefulness to the nation, and in the War of 1812, with its swift mingling of the men of the State and its soldierly discipline, we find *the first internal cause* of the remarkable upbuilding of her people's power, soon to be made variously evident.

A second cause of Ohio's rapid rise in political power was the really wonderful development of a moral tone of profound earnestness in their political principles which gradually came to dominate the mass of the people. This began with the planting of the antislavery doctrine, the propagation of which was, owing to the operation of selection through the Ordinance of 1787, pushed forward fully as much by Ohioans of Southern as by Ohioans of Northern or New England birth. It was to have been expected under any circumstances that the New England settlements would have their agitators like Charles B. Storrs, the President of Hudson College, in the Western Reserve, its Finney, and "Father" Keep, and Fairchild, its

Ohio's Ascendency Analyzed

firebrand John Brown, and its political warriors Giddings and Wade. It was to have been expected that Pennsylvania would furnish its Quaker abolitionists, like Achilles Pugh, and New Jersey its Benjamin Lundy, but that Virginia and Kentucky and the Carolinas should have supplied an equal, or a superior contingent, to the forefront of the fight against slavery, can only be accounted for on the ground that the "Ordinance of Freedom" was one of the most perfect working and beneficently effective pieces of moral and legal machinery ever evolved from the mind of man. The New England and Pennsylvania and New Jersey antislavery men simply "went West" on the indicated path of empire, but the Southern-born friends of freedom were diverted from the natural path of immigration, as if by a magnetic attraction, and instead of becoming Kentuckians or Tennesseeans, they helped to found Ohio, and to foster, even more than the Northerners, a great colony favorable to freedom, vitally progressive and aggressive, and finally victorious.

Clermont County, on the Ohio River, and its neighborhood, settled by Virginians,

Ohio and Her Western Reserve

was as strong an antislavery citadel as was the Reserve, on Lake Erie, settled by Connecticut and Massachusetts men. Gatch and Sergent, who were its delegates to the Constitutional Convention of 1802, were elected "because they were Virginians, the strongest of antislavery men, and practical emancipators." Here, too, came the Rev. John Rankin from Tennessee, Obed Denham, of Virginia, and that superb national leader of antislavery, James G. Birney, who was twice the candidate of the Liberty party for the Presidency of the United States, from Kentucky—all because they abhorred slavery and sought a home where it was prohibited. And here came Thomas Morris, of Massachusetts descent, to be sure, though his mother was a Virginian, who, like other settlers from the

Ohio's Ascendency Analyzed

South, had to attest a love for freedom by relinquishing the slaves she inherited; and Morris—as one of the very first champions of freedom in the United States Senate, answering Calhoun's and Clay's pleadings for the "peculiar institution," and electrifying the Senate and nation by the prediction that the negro should be free—was simply the voice of the virile sentiment of those Southern antislavery men in Ohio.

It was through the molding effect of the early, persistent, unremitting antislavery agitation, and the very fact that it had the Southerners as well as the Northerners among its foremost champions and strongest supporters, that there was developed that preponderating and tremendously vigorous moral sentiment which penetrated the masses, and making Ohio the force that it was in the war of the rebellion, established its high prestige in the nation.

It was a full generation from the first antislavery agitation in pioneer Ohio to the days of the civil war in which its tremendous progress became apparent. In the meantime, the forces of the ordinance, of Gallatin's great internal-

Ohio and Her Western Reserve

improvements measure, of popular education, and of public works, had been furthering the population, prosperity, and general moral as well as material well-being of the State. It had progressed from a trifle over 42,000 population and eighteenth place in rank, at the time of its founding, to 230,760 and thirteenth place in 1810; to 581,295 and fifth place in 1820; to 937,903 in 1830; to 1,519,467 and third place in 1840; to 1,980,329 in 1850; and to a population of 2,339,511 in 1860—still holding third place in the sisterhood of States—and destined to hold it for thirty years more.

CHAPTER XI

OHIO IN THE WAR AND IN CIVIL LIFE

WHEN the civil war came it would seem as if the sapience of statesmen, the labors of legislators, the forces of man, and the circumstances of time and nature—the drift of destiny—had all been directed toward the sole result of building up Ohio as a fortress for the Union, at the very place where the loyal land was narrowest, between armed rebellion and British territory. There was no nobler showing of stamina and strength than hers. She resisted invasion, helped to create, raise up, and protect a loyal State upon her border, and sent into the strife enough men to constitute a vast army of her own, more than half of her adult population, half again larger than the greatest army Great Britain ever put in the field, and one-ninth of the entire Federal force engaged in the war—a total of 340,000

Ohio and Her Western Reserve

men, or, reduced to a three years' basis, 240,000 men. Her total dead (24,564) were 4,000 in excess of all losses on both sides in the Revolutionary War.

But not less indicative of Ohio's service in the war for the Union than her numbers was the length of her officers' list and the distinction of its *personnel*.

Of commanding generals belonging to Ohio there were, first of all, Ulysses S. Grant, born at Mount Pleasant, Clermont County, April 27, 1822; William Tecumseh Sherman, born in Lancaster, 1820; and Philip H. Sheridan, born in Albany, N. Y., but brought in infancy to Somerset, Perry County, Ohio. Of major-generals born in the State and entering the service from it there were thirteen—viz.,

Ohio in the War and in Civil Life

Don Carlos Buell, George Crook, George A. Custer, Quincy A. Gillmore, James A. Garfield, James B. McPherson, Irvin McDowell, Alexander McD. McCook, William S. Rosecrans (born in Kingston, Ohio, 1819), David S. Stanley, Robert C. Schenck, John Wager Swayne, and Godfrey Weitzel. Of the brigadier-generals of Ohio birth who went from the State there were thirty-five (many of them brevetted major-generals)—viz., William T. H. Brooks, William W. Burns, Henry B. Banning, C. P. Buckingham, John Beatty, Joel A. Dewey, Thomas H. Ewing, Hugh B. Ewing, James W. Forsythe, Robert S. Granger, Kenner Garrard, Charles Griffin, Rutherford B. Hayes, J. Warren Keifer, William H. Lytle, John S. Lee, John S. Mason, Robert L. McCook, Daniel McCook, John G. Mitchell, Nathaniel C. McLean, Emerson Opdycke, Benjamin F. Potts, A. Sanders Piatt, James

Ohio and Her Western Reserve

S. Robinson, Benjamin P. Runkle, J. W. Reilly, William Sooy Smith, Joshua Sill, John P. Slough, Ferdinand Van DeVeer, Charles R. Woods, Willard Warner, William B. Woods, Charles C. Wolcutt, and M. S. Wade. But this by no means tells the story of all that the State is entitled to, for there should be included a number, smaller than the native-born but still a considerable showing, of those who though born elsewhere were residents of the State. Of such were Major-Generals Jacob D. Cox and M. D. Leggett (New York), William B. Hazen (Vermont), George B. McClellan and Jacob D. Steedman (Pennsylvania), O. M. Mitchell (Kentucky); and of Brigadiers Jacob Ammen, B. W. Brice, and John S. Tibball (Virginia), Samuel

Ohio in the War and in Civil Life

Beatty and George W. Morgan (Pennsylvania), Ralph P. Buckland and Thomas Kilbey Smith (Massachusetts), H. B. Carrington (Connecticut), George P. Este (New Hampshire), Manning F. Force (Washington, D.C.), John W. Fuller (England), Charles W. Hill (Vermont), August V. Kautz (Germany), E. P. Scammon (Maine), John W. Sprague and Erastus B. Tyler (New York), and August Willich (Prussia).

It is obviously unfair, having followed the foregoing basis of classification, to lay claim to the generals of Ohio birth who at the time of entering the service were residents of other States, but if such were included, the list would be swelled by the names of Benjamin Harrison, of Indiana; Halbert E. Paine, of Wisconsin; Eleazar A. Paine, of the regular army; Robert B. Mitch-

Ohio and Her Western Reserve

ell, of Kansas; and others. Ohio also made two notable contributions to the navy, Admiral Daniel Ammen and Rear-Admiral Joseph N. Miller.

On the civil side, both in the State and in the nation, Ohio was not a less forceful or effective factor in the subduing of rebellion than upon the military. Her "war Governors"—Dennison, Tod, and Brough—were any and all worthy to stand between Morton in the West and Curtin and Dix in the East. The fact that Tod and Brough were Democrats, though elected on the "Union" ticket, was perhaps more indicative of the practical wholeness of Ohio's loyalism than if they had been Republicans. Brough's opponent was Clement L. Vallandigham. There was a rousing campaign, which resulted in the triumphant election of "rough, bluff John Brough" by the then unprecedented majority of over 100,000 votes. The issue had been distinctly "the vigorous prosecution of the war," and the position of Ohio was most emphatically declared. John Sherman is on record as pronouncing the election of Brough as an important influence in favor of the

Ohio in the War and in Civil Life

Union cause, and "equal to that of any battle of the war."

Ohio in the conduct of the war at Washington, however, far more than equaled Ohio at Columbus; for there stood next to Lincoln Stanton and Chase, Wade, Sherman, and Jay Cooke.

Of the eight Ohioans who were colossal powers on the civil side of the service for the Union, all but two were native-born. Salmon P. Chase, who had been Governor of the State and Senator of the United States, was  Secretary of the Treasury during nearly the whole of the war period—that is, from March, 1861, to March, 1864; and Benjamin F. Wade, long time Senator, became chairman of the Committee on the Conduct of the War, in which capacity his service was invaluable. Chase was born in New Hampshire and Wade in Massachusetts, but both came to Ohio in their

Ohio and Her Western Reserve

very early years. The six others whose services were in importance fully abreast of these were Ohio-born. First of all, perhaps, was the stern, unflinching Edwin M. Stanton (born at Steubenville, 1814), who was Secretary of War from January, 1862, until August, 1867. John Sherman (born at Lancaster) was the controlling member of the Finance Committee of the Senate. Jay Cooke (born at Sandusky) was special agent of the United States Treasury Department for the negotiation of bonds. As to the three "war Governors," they were from three extreme corners of the State—William Dennison, born at Cincinnati; David Tod, born at Youngstown; and John Brough, born at Marietta.

Edwin M. Stanton

The time had come in the war for the backwoods to bourgeon, and for the seed sown and nurtured in the wilderness by the nation

"These are my Jewels."

"Favorite Sons" Monument in Capitol grounds at Columbus.

Ohio in the War and in Civil Life

to bear its first great fruit. No State has had more numerous or more notably useful "favorite sons," and none has been more frankly proud of them. Ohio points to the Presidents and statesmen and great generals she has reared with the conscious and consummate pride of the Roman matron, in alluding to her sons, saying with her, "*These are my Jewels*"; and she has inscribed this legend upon a noble monument erected to their memory in the Capitol grounds at Columbus.

Ohio went splendidly to the front in the military service of the nation, and it has remained pretty solidly at the front in the conduct of civil affairs for more than a generation. The State, which had been built by the nation, had proved one of the firmest fortresses of the nation in the time of its siege and assault, and now it began to contribute freely of its best product, its native-born sons, to the councils and the supreme control of the country at large. It was a case of the child long cared for and cherished coming in maturity to be the staff and support of the sire.

The State, to be sure, had contributed a

Ohio and Her Western Reserve

President in 1840, and its first Cabinet member as early as 1814; but she now gave the country three Presidents in succession and Cabinet officers in profusion, to say nothing of hosts of lesser officials, at the same time maintaining, by the high ability and sterling character of her delegates, that conspicuity which long before the war had attached to Ohio in Congress.

While Ohio was strongly in evidence at Washington nearly all the time for forty years, there were special periods when the prevalency of the Buckeye man was particularly noticeable and a source of pride to her people and of mingled amusement and mild irritation to the remainder of the United States. The time when Garfield came to the presidency (1881) was one of these periods of predominancy which circumstances conspired to make extra conspicuous. The men made prominent by the war had not yet reached retirement, and the civilians had come to keep them company. Just as Garfield was about to leave Mentor for the inauguration he remarked tentatively to a New York politician, "I suppose Ohio has received about all she is

Ohio in the War and in Civil Life

entitled to?" to which the Eastern man answered sententiously, "She's got as much as the other States will stand, at any rate." The scene at the inauguration was of a nature to substantiate this view. There were gathered on the east portico of the Capitol, in a compact group, the principal characters of the day—the retiring President, Rutherford B. Hayes, of Ohio! the President about to be inducted into office, James A. Garfield, of Ohio! the Chief Justice of the Supreme Court, who administered the oath of office, Morrison R. Waite, of Ohio! while close by them, as the most-honored spectators, stood the Secretary of the Treasury, John Sherman, of Ohio! next to him the General of the Army, William T. Sherman, of Ohio! and by his side the second in command, Lieutenant-General Sheridan, of Ohio!

Almost any time during the subsequent decade the Ohioans were to be found in good force at the front in all branches of the Government, and in 1886, in conformance with this general predominance of her sons, could have been observed the rather startling fact that the State had no less than ten Senators

Ohio and Her Western Reserve

in the higher house of the national Legislature. There were two as her very own regularly elected members, and no less than eight accredited to various farther Western States, but all born in Ohio, and ready to a man to stand by her interests. The House of Representatives at the same time held some forty or fifty Ohio-born Congressmen—about half of whom went from Ohio districts, and the others from constituencies in Indiana, Illinois, Iowa, Kansas, and various States, which it was now most pertinently made manifest Ohio had been helping to build.

But the most surprising and amusing evidence of the Ohio man's ubiquitousness came at the close of this same decade, when Benjamin Harrison, a citizen of Indiana, born in Ohio, assumed the duties of the presidency of March 4, 1889. The nation felt relieved when his Cabinet was announced, for instead of the Ohioans, who had been overwhelmingly predominant under most former administrations for thirty years, appeared such men as Windom, of Minnesota; W. H. H. Miller, of Indiana; John W. Noble, of Missouri; Jeremiah M. Rusk, of Wisconsin; and (later)

Ohio in the War and in Civil Life

Stephen B. Elkins, of West Virginia. But lo, this was only a most superficial pretense of avoiding the Buckeye as material for Cabinet-making, for every man of them was born an Ohioan! And Charles Foster, who was an undisguised Ohio man, had a place later, making this altogether the strongest Ohio Cabinet of the whole series.

Some idea of the full fruition of Ohio in a political sense during the prolific *post-bellum* period, and that of lesser outcome before the war, is afforded by a summary of her offerings to high officialdom, which have included six Presidents if we count William Henry Harrison (1841) born in Virginia, or five if we count only those native to the State: Ulysses S. Grant, 1869-'77; Rutherford B. Hayes, 1877-'81; James A. Garfield, 1881; Benjamin Harrison, 1889-'93; William McKinley, 1897-1901, and 1901, March 4 to September 14. One Vice-President, Thomas A. Hendricks, 1885. Three presidents of the Senate (*pro tem.*), viz., Benjamin F. Wade, Allen G. Thurman, John Sherman. Seven Justices of the Supreme Court, two of them Chief Justices, viz., Salmon P. Chase (Chief

Ohio and Her Western Reserve

Justice), 1864–'73; Morrison R. Waite (Chief Justice), 1874–'87; Noah H. Swayne, 1862–'81; Edwin M. Stanton, 1869; Stanley J. Matthews, 1881–'89; William B. Woods, 1880–'87. Two Secretaries of State: John Sherman, William R. Day. Six Secretaries of the Treasury: Ewing, Corwin, Chase, Sherman, Windom, and Foster. Seven Secretaries of War: McLean, Stanton, Grant, Sherman, Taft, Elkins, and Alger. Four Secretaries of the Interior: Ewing, Cox, Delano, Noble. Five Attorney-Generals: Stanberry, Taft, Stanton, Miller, and Harmon. Four Postmasters-General: Meigs, McLean, Dennison, Hatton. And one Secretary of Agriculture, Rusk.

The large extent to which the Cabinets have been built of Buckeye timber is far better revealed by the following list, arranged chronologically by administrations:

Administration of James Madison, 1809–'17: Postmaster-General, Return Jonathan Meigs, March 17, 1814.

Administration of James Monroe, 1817–'25: Postmaster-General, R. J. Meigs (reappointed); John McLean, June 26, 1823.

Ohio in the War and in Civil Life

Administrations of William Henry Harrison, 1841, and John Tyler, 1841–'45: Secretary of the Treasury, Thomas Ewing, March 5, 1841; Secretary of War, John McLean, September 13, 1841.

Administrations of Zachary Taylor, 1849–'50, and Millard Fillmore, 1850–'53: Secretary of the Treasury, Thomas Corwin, July 23, 1850; Secretary of the Interior, Thomas H. Ewing, March 8, 1849.

Administration of James Buchanan, 1857–'60: Attorney-General, Edwin M. Stanton (born in Ohio, appointed from Pennsylvania), December 20, 1860.

Administrations of Abraham Lincoln, 1861–'65, and Andrew Johnson, 1865–'69: Secretary of the Treasury, Salmon P. Chase, March 5, 1861; Secretary of War, Edwin M. Stanton, January 15, 1862; U. S. Grant (*ad interim*), August 12, 1867; Edwin M. Stanton (reinstated), January 14, 1868, to May 28, 1868; Attorney-General, Henry Stanberry, July 23, 1866, to July 15, 1868; Postmaster-General, William Dennison, September 24, 1864, to July 25, 1866.

Administration of Ulysses S. Grant, 1869–

Ohio and Her Western Reserve

'77 : Secretary of War, William T. Sherman, September 9, 1869, to October 25, 1869; Alphonso Taft, March 8, 1876, to May 8, 1876; Secretary of the Interior, Jacob D. Cox, March 5, 1869, to November 1, 1870; Columbus Delano, November 1, 1870, to October 19, 1875; Attorney-General, Alphonso Taft, May 22, 1876.

Administration of Rutherford B. Hayes, 1877–'81; Secretary of the Treasury, John Sherman, March 8, 1877.

Administrations of James A. Garfield, 1881, and Chester A. Arthur, 1881–'85: Secretary of the Treasury, William Windom (born in Ohio, appointed from Minnesota), March 5, 1881, to October 27, 1882; Postmaster-General, Frank Hatton (born in Ohio, appointed from Iowa), October 14, 1884.

Administration of Benjamin Harrison, 1889–'93: Secretary of the Treasury, William Windom (born in Ohio, appointed from Minnesota), reappointed March 7, 1889; Charles Foster, February 21, 1891; Secretary of War, Stephen B. Elkins (born in Ohio, appointed from West Virginia), December 4, 1891, to March 6, 1893; Attorney-General,

Ohio in the War and in Civil Life

W. H. H. Miller (born in Ohio, appointed from Indiana), March 7, 1889; Secretary of the Interior, John W. Noble (born in Ohio, appointed from Missouri), March 7, 1889; Secretary of Agriculture, Jeremiah M. Rusk (born in Ohio, appointed from Wisconsin), March 7, 1889.

Administration of Grover Cleveland, 1893–'97: Attorney-General, Judson Harmon, June 7, 1895, to March 5, 1897.

Administration of William McKinley, 1897–1901, 1901: Secretary of State, John Sherman, March 5, 1897, to April 26, 1898; William Rufus Day (former Assistant Secretary), April 26, 1898, to September 30, 1898 (resigned); Secretary of War, Russell A. Alger (born in Ohio, appointed from Michigan), March 5, 1897, to August 1, 1899 (resigned).

Besides these there are, of course, a very large number of assistant secretaries and bureau chiefs; and the State's phenomenal productivity of men fitted for public duty has been constantly attested by the presence of Ohioans in high diplomatic positions; but the limitations of this volume preclude men-

Ohio and Her Western Reserve

tion of them, and in pursuance of the original purpose of showing the character rather than the full extent of Ohio's contribution to the public service of the nation, the presentation must be confined to those only who have occupied the very highest offices.*

OHIO IN THE NATION'S SENATE

Following is a list of the Ohio members of the United States Senate, preceded by the

---

* A certain luster, too, has been reflected upon the State by those of her citizens who have found honor far beyond her borders, as, for instance, Samuel Sullivan ("Sunset") Cox, who successively represented Ohio and New York in Congress and the United States as Minister to Turkey; Senators Julius Cæsar Burrows, of Michigan; Daniel W. Voorhees, Joseph E. McDonald, David Turpie, and C. W. Fairbanks, of Indiana; William B. Allison and James F. Wilson, of Iowa; Preston B. Plumb, of Kansas; Thomas H. Carter, of Montana; and William M. Stewart, of Nevada.

And besides these, there can be mentioned as Ohioans who have performed important service the late General James M. Ruggles, of Illinois, one of the committee (the others being Abraham Lincoln and Ebenezer Peck) who drafted the platform on which the Republican party was organized, and General James W. Denver, after whom Denver, Col., was named, afterward Governor of Kansas, as was Thomas Carney, in war times, and Lyman U. Humphrey. Later still, another Ohioan who became a Western Governor was G. P. Morehouse (Missouri); and at the same time Iowa had an Ohio man—J. H. Rothneck—as its Supreme Judge.

Ohio in the War and in Civil Life

delegates under the brief second stage of Territorial government:

OHIO DELEGATES TO UNITED STATES CONGRESS

William Henry Harrison (Hamilton County), 1799–1801.

William McMillan (Hamilton County), 1799–1801.

Paul Fearing (Washington County), 1801–1803.

UNITED STATES SENATORS FROM OHIO

Thomas Worthington (Ross County), 1803–'09. Reelected 1809 to serve to 1815. Resigned December 8, 1810, to accept the office of Governor.

John Smith (Hamilton County), 1803. Resigned.

Edward Tiffin (Ross County), 1807–'11.

Return Jonathan Meigs (Washington County), 1807–'11 (*vice* Smith, resigned).

Alexander Campbell (Brown County), 1809–'13.

Stanley Griswold (Cuyahoga County), 1809–'11.

Jeremiah Morrow (Warren), 1813–'19.

Ohio and Her Western Reserve

Joseph Kerr (Ross County) (*vice* Worthington, resigned).

Benjamin Ruggles (Belmont), 1815–'33.

William Trimble (Highland), 1819–'23. (Died 1822 from the effects of a wound received at battle of Fort Erie, 1812.)

Ethan A. Brown (Hamilton County), 1822–'25 (*vice* Trimble, deceased).

William Henry Harrison (Hamilton County), 1825–'29. (Resigned 1828, to accept appointment as Minister to Colombia.)

Jacob Burnet (Hamilton County), 1827–'31 (*vice* Harrison, resigned).

Thomas Ewing (Fairfield County), 1831–'37. Reelected for term 1849–'51 (*vice* Corwin, deceased).

Thomas Morris (Clermont), 1833–'39.

William Allen (Ross County), 1837–'49.

Benjamin Tappan (Jefferson County), 1839–'45.

Thomas Corwin (Warren County), 1845–'49. Died 1849, previous to convening of Thirty-first Congress, to which he was elected.

Salmon P. Chase (Hamilton), 1849–'55. Reelected 1863. (Resigned to accept appointment as Secretary of the Treasury.)

Ohio in the War and in Civil Life

Benjamin F. Wade (Ashtabula), 1851–1869.

George E. Pugh (Hamilton), 1855–'61.

John Sherman* (Richland), 1861–'77. Resigned 1877 to accept appointment as Secretary of United States Treasury. Reelected 1881. March, 1897.

James A. Garfield (Lake County), January 11, 1880. (Declined the office January 18, 1881, having in the meantime been elected President.)

Allen G. Thurman (Franklin County), 1869–'81.

Stanley Matthews (Hamilton County), 1877–'79 (*vice* Sherman, resigned).

George H. Pendleton (Hamilton County), 1879–'85.

Henry B. Payne (Cuyahoga County), 1885–'91.

---

* John Sherman's first service, from March 23, 1861, to March 8, 1877, made 15 years, 11 months, 15 days. Entering again March 4, 1881, he had on June 16, 1894, surpassed the term of Thomas H. Benton (December 6, 1821, to March 3, 1851, 29 years, 2 months, 27 days). From that time on his service was in excess of Benton's 2 years, 8 months, and 16 days, or a total service of 31 years, 11 months, and 13 days in the United States Senate.

Ohio and Her Western Reserve

Joseph B. Foraker (Hamilton County), 1897–1903.

Marcus A. Hanna (Cuyahoga), 1899–1905.

Governors of the State

1803. Edward Tiffin, Ross County, three years and a half.
1807. Thomas Kirker, Adams County (appointed), six months.
1808. Samuel Huntington, Trumbull County, two years.
1810. Return Jonathan Meigs, Washington County, three years and a half.
1814. Othniel Looker, Hamilton County, six months.
1814. Thomas Worthington, Ross County, two years.
1818. Ethan A. Brown, Hamilton County, three years and a half.
1822. Allen Trimble, Highland County, six months.
1822. Jeremiah Morrow, Warren County, four years.
1826. Allen Trimble, Highland County, four years.

Ohio in the War and in Civil Life

1830. Duncan McArthur, Ross County, two years.
1832. Robert Lucas, Pipe County, four years.
1836. Joseph Vance, Champaign County, two years.
1838. Wilson Shannon, Belmont County, two years.
1840. Thomas Corwin, Warren County, two years.
1842. Wilson Shannon, Belmont County, one year and a half.
1844. Thomas W. Bartley, Richland County, six months.
1846. William Bebb, Butler County, two years.
1848. Seabury Ford, Geauga County, one year and eleven months.
1850. Reuben Wood, Cuyahoga County, one year and a half.
1853. William Medill, Fairfield County, two years and a half.
1855. Salmon P. Chase, Hamilton County, four years.
1859. William Dennison, Franklin County, two years.
1861. David Tod, Mahoning County, two years.

Ohio and Her Western Reserve

1863. John Brough, Cuyahoga County, one year and seven months.
1865. Charles Anderson, Montgomery County, five months.
1865. Jacob Dolson Cox, Trumbull County, two years.
1867. Rutherford Birchard Hayes, Hamilton County, four years.
1871. Edward F. Noyes, Hamilton County, two years.
1873. William Allen, Ross County, two years.
1875. Rutherford Birchard Hayes, Sandusky County, a year and three months.
1877. Thomas L. Young, Hamilton County, six months.
1877. R. M. Bishop, Hamilton County, two years.
1880. Charles Foster, Seneca County, four years.
1883. George Hoadley, Hamilton County, two years.
1885. Joseph B. Foraker, Hamilton County, four years.
1890. James E. Campbell, Butler County, two years.

Ohio in the War and in Civil Life

1892. William McKinley, Stark County, four years.
1895. Asa Smith Bushnell, Clarke County, four years.
1899. George Kilbon Nash, Franklin County —reelected 1901—present incumbent of office.

But it is not alone in politics, but in the world of science, literature, journalism, and art that Ohio has been phenomenally prolific in her forthputtings. More noise has been made about the "Hoosiers," but the native "Buckeye" authors of recognized standing outnumber them more than three to one. Indiana is accredited with 55, Illinois with 47, Michigan with 36, but Ohio has a roster of 174 names, or only seven less than those of the three States named, and all of the other Western States combined. Since the days of Otway Curry and Alice and Phœbe Cary there have been among them many votaries of the Muse, of whom the most prominent (not to mention William A. Gallagher and Coates Kinney, commonly attributed to Ohio because of long association, but not na-

Ohio and Her Western Reserve

tives) have been the Piatts, General Lytle, and Miss Edith Thomas. Of course, William D. Howells stands out first of all in anybody's recalling of Ohio authors; but there are many others of fine quality, if of less universal renown, as A. P. Russell, A. J. Fullerton (who sent to the Atlantic the first literary contribution from the West), Delia Bacon (of Bacon-Shakespeare fame), Ambrose Bierce, Judge Tourgee, George Kennan, Prof. George T. Ladd, Thomas Jay Hudson, Sarah C. Woolsey (Susan Coolidge), William H. Venable, Thomas Donaldson, Paul Laurence Dunbar, Mary Hartley Catherwood, Nathaniel Stephenson, and Alfred Henry Lewis. But when we have mentioned these we have not yet included a single one of the historians, who are perhaps the class most conspicuous in Ohio authorship. First among them was Hubert Howe Bancroft, the historian of the Pacific Slope; and the greatest of those now living is James Ford Rhodes. Two others who are well known are Prof. William M. Sloane, of Princeton (author of a Life of Napoleon and a History of the French and Indian War and the Revolution), and

Ohio in the War and in Civil Life

Prof. Edwin Erl Sparks, of the University of Illinois, author of American Expansion. Hildreth, Rufus King, and the late Burke A. Hinsdale have all performed valuable service in this field.

Just where journalism and literature meet stands an Ohio man—Albert Shaw, editor of the American Review of Reviews; and in journalism pure and simple and at its best strength there stands a larger host than we can even mention. But it is a curious circumstance that for a considerable period three of the great metropolitan dailies were simultaneously managed by three Ohio journalists: The Tribune by Whitelaw Reid, the World by John A. Cockerill, the Herald by Julius Chambers. Two other journalists the State contributed to New York—Murat Halstead, and Adolph S. Ochs, proprietor of the Times. But besides these and the peerless MacGahan, and such brilliant world-known correspondents as E. V. Smalley and H. V. Boynton, there were Richard Smith, G. M. D. Bloss, and Frederick Haussureck, of Cincinnati; Joseph Medill and Alfred Cowles, of Chicago; also the late Edwin

Ohio and Her Western Reserve

Cowles, the long-time editor of the Cleveland Leader.

As to art, it was an Ohioan who first gave American art a prestige abroad—Hiram Powers. Another Ohioan, John Quincy Adams Ward, became the first sculptor of America. Thomas Cole became one of the country's greatest landscape painters and engravers. James H. and William H. Beard by their originality in art achieved national and international reputation, and the art world well knows to-day the work of Kenyon Cox, Frank Duvaneck, W. H. Powell, A. S. Wyant, W. L. Sontag, Frank Dangler, Wilson McDonald, T. D. Jones, William Walcutt, Henry Mosler, Caroline S. Brooks, E. M. Ward, F. C. Webber, Jasper Lanman, John Henry Witt, Marion Foster, J. H. Twatchman, and Frank H. Tompkins.

In physical science there shine such Ohio names as those of Ormsby M. Mitchell, Wormely, Sullivant, Newberry, Kirtland, Wright; while those of Elisha Gray, Charles Francis Brush, and Thomas Alva Edison as pioneers in the practical application of advanced science are of universal renown.

CHAPTER XII

SUMMARY AND CONCLUSION

As for the causes of the remarkable putting forth of political fruit by the Buckeye tree, it must be borne in mind that the war itself was a powerful stimulus to the spirit of the people, and in addition to the influence of the Ordinance, of Gallatin's pioneer internal-improvement measure, of geographical position, and of the energy derived from the mingling of widely differing elements of population which had made the Ohioans a numerically great and phenomenally strong race—other agencies were working which had a more particular effect on the constitution of political power than those mentioned.

First of all, Ohio was, through a seeming paradox—which is superficial and simply enough explained—a persistent and enormous

Ohio and Her Western Reserve

power in the electoral strife of the nation, for the very reason that she was never in her period of primacy, so overwhelmingly partizan as to make it absolutely sure which way her vote would be cast. As has already been shown, the Jeffersonians, who brought the State into being, held its mastery for twenty years. It voted for Clay in 1824. Then, with the reorganization of parties, it became less stable. It voted for Jackson and Carr, Democrats, respectively, in 1828 and 1832; for Harrison and Clay, Whigs, in 1836, 1840, and 1844; then for Cass and Pierce, Democrats, in 1848 and 1852. In 1856 it voted for Frémont, and ever since the Republicans have had the benefit of its franchise. But Ohio had a way between times of letting a Democrat assume the toga of the governorship, two of her three great war Governors being Democrats (though elected on a Union or fusion platform), and, on the average, one out of every four governors since then being of the minority party. This uncertainty as to outcome at any given time, based on the independent habit of mind of a large contingent of her citizens, made it worth while—

Summary and Conclusion

especially in view of Ohio's size in the electoral college—to consult the preferences of her people in national campaigns, and often to make sure of their suffrage by the naming of a local candidate. The converse of this condition is clearly exhibited in Ohio's next-door neighbor on the east, which, though giving with unvarying certainty overwhelmingly great predetermined majorities, has been accorded but one nomination for the office of Chief Executive in half a century.

The factitious but effective force brought to bear on the foregoing situation, by the consideration that Ohio was an "October State," considerably enhanced her power. The "closeness" of the issue, or the comparatively even matching of parties, and the fact that all her State battles were eagerly watched by the whole nation, gave them an importance which variously redounded to the State's political advantage.

But a far more effective, though less theatric, source of Ohio's strength in national politics lay in the manner in which she sustained in public life and in official position those men whose preeminent fitness once be-

Ohio and Her Western Reserve

came demonstrated. In this policy she has only been equaled by New England and certain sections of the South. Thus her statesmen had opportunity to carry out, through the advantages of familiarity with their surroundings and of prolonged and purposeful study afforded by their continuance in office by wise constituents, those settled policies and plans which alike conferred honor upon themselves and the State. A swift glance over the records of Ohio's leading Representatives and Senators affords abundant confirmation of the claim of frequency of long terms accorded them. James M. Ashley, a colleague (and able coworker for the same causes) of Giddings, served ten years as Representative; John A. Bingham, writer of the fourteenth amendment to the Constitution, sixteen years; Benjamin Butterworth, ten; Thomas Corwin, fourteen in the House and four in the Senate (dying before his term expired), eighteen years in all; Columbus Delano, twenty-two; Giddings, twenty-two; Garfield, seventeen (being then in quick succession elected to the Senate and the presidency); McKinley, fourteen (ended only by his choice as Chief

Summary and Conclusion

Executive); Jeremiah Morrow (of early days), nineteen (in House and Senate); Joseph Vance, eighteen; Samuel F. Vinton, twenty; Robert C. Schenck, sixteen. In the Senate we find Benjamin Ruggles serving continuously seventeen years; William Allen, twelve; Benjamin F. Wade, eighteen; Allen G. Thurman, twelve; and John Sherman, surpassing in his total term not only all Ohio records, but all in the history of the Senate, even that of Thomas H. Benton, and having to his credit almost thirty-two years (thirty-one years and about eleven and a half months) in this station, and enough more in other high office to make a total of half a century of exalted public service.

A still further source of Ohio's primacy in broadly public affairs must be looked for in those mingled feelings of strong State pride and of sturdy, dignifying nationalism, which have come naturally, and almost insensibly, to animate its people. She had attained third place as to population twenty years before the war, and she held it for thirty years after, only surrendering it in 1890 to Illinois (which is as much larger,

Ohio and Her Western Reserve

territorially, as is eight larger than five), advancing in population in the meantime from 2,309,511 in 1860 to 2,665,260 in 1870; to 3,198,062 in 1880; to 3,672,376 in 1890; and to 4,157,545 in 1900. But her rank was not dependent on numbers alone. For many years she was also third among the States in wealth. She was long first, and subsequently second, in the value of farms and farm improvements. She was for years, and is now, fourth in the total value of mineral products, and third in the production of coal, being exceeded only by Pennsylvania and Illinois. She is ranked as fifth in manufactures. And in education and religion she very naturally is one of the foremost States in the Union. But with all of the growth thus represented, and having increased her population in an even hundred years one thousand fold, Ohio had early begun to build other States in the West. Her sons were among the Argonauts in California in the mid-century, and they have been among the pioneers of all the States ever since. She has undoubtedly contributed to them fully 2,000,000 people, and more than half of that number born in Ohio

Summary and Conclusion

are now living in the Western commonwealths.*

---

* As a matter of fact, the total number of people born in Ohio, but contributed to, and in 1900 living in, other States or Territories, was 1,114,165. The largest numbers, as might be expected, are to be found in Indiana, Illinois, Kansas, Iowa, Missouri, and Michigan, but the number of Ohioans living in most of these Western States was not so large in 1900 as in 1880, while, on the other hand, in the twenty intervening years, the migration into States lying easterly has very considerably increased—noticeably that into New York and Pennsylvania. The following table of the Ohio-born in the States where they are most numerous reveals the figures for 1880 and 1900, and is interestingly indicative of some curious movements in the tides of population, as well as valuable in showing the extent to which Ohio has been a builder of other States:

	1880.	1900.		1880.	1900.
Indiana	186,391	178,344	Pennsylvania	27,502	57,436
Illinois	136,884	137,161	New York	11,599	26,219
Iowa	120,495	88,146	Wisconsin	20,512	19,036
Kansas	93,396	88,298	California	17,759	34,869
Missouri	78,938	80,966	Minnesota	15,560	18,971
Michigan	77,053	88,290	Colorado	11,759	24,894
Nebraska	31,800	40,981	Texas	7,949	10,588
W. Virginia.	27,535	40,301	Oregon	6,201	13,123
Kentucky	27,115	38,539			

Of the other Western States, Washington leads with 16,762 Ohioans (in 1900); North and South Dakota have respectively 4,391 and 7,106; Montana has 6,650; Wyoming, 3,336; Idaho, 3,815; New Mexico, 1,768; Arizona, 2,100; Utah, 2,525; Arkansas, 8,867; Indian Territory, 3,392; Nevada, least of all, 741; and Oklahoma, 15,049.

Of the Southern States, Tennessee (next to Kentucky and West Virginia) had in 1900 the largest number of natives of

Ohio and Her Western Reserve

Ohio, by her vast growth in population, by the multiform character as well as the magnitude of her national development, by the effectiveness of the exertion of her enor-

Ohio, 10,353. Alabama had 4,029; Mississippi, 1,538; Louisiana, 2,545; Virginia, 3,799; District of Columbia, 4,348; Maryland, 3,204; Georgia, 2,542; Florida, 2,721; and the remaining States much smaller numbers.

The New England States, which contributed largely to the upbuilding of Ohio, have received something of the reflex tide. Massachusetts led in 1900 with 5,353 Ohioans, and Connecticut had 2,230.

New Jersey had 5,553.

Of States contributing to Ohio, as shown by their native-born living there in 1900, Pennsylvania was naturally the leader. The figures for the principal ones, in order of the number of their native-born in Ohio, are as follows:

Pennsylvania	131,142	Massachusetts	7,507
New York	56,652	New Jersey	7,070
Kentucky	53,464	Iowa	6,805
Indiana	52,045	Tennessee	5,893
Virginia	32,342	Kansas	5,325
Michigan	31,356	Connecticut	4,467
West Virginia	30,524	Wisconsin	4,320
Illinois	18,964	North Carolina	3,407
Maryland	13,212	Vermont	3,553
Missouri	7,591		

Foreign countries' contributions of late years are headed by Germany, of whose people 204,160 were living in Ohio in 1900. There were of Irish nativity at the same time, 55,018; of English, 44,745; and of Canadians—English, 19,864, and French, 2,903. The total foreign-born population was 458,734, or 11 per cent of Ohio's 4,157,545 people.

Summary and Conclusion

mous strength for the Union, and by the exercise and outcome of her influence upon the nation, long ago arrived at that dignity of position which is claimed in the matter of her State seal, of being literally an empire within an empire—"*Imperium in imperio.*" And thus, located in the middle country, looking westward to the homes of her sons, and eastward to those of her sires, the horizon of her interest and her influence is broadened to the bounds of the Union itself; and while contemplating her own achievements, and feeling her own strength—of which she first became fully conscious in the period of the civil war—she turns reverently the page of history, to be reminded that she is the creature of the nation; that her foundations were lain by the people of *all* the States, that her existence was decreed and directed by the legal enactments of the nation, and that she was in fact the first product of nationalism.

Hence nationalism, which is the outgrowth of a larger conception of citizenship, represents a robust element in the Ohioan's mood of mind. But with his profound patriotism there must be ever a place, too, for a

Ohio and Her Western Reserve

passionate, insistent State pride. The very fact that circumstances have never called for choice, or division, between the two, makes the dual allegiance one of doubly strong devotion.

The subject of the Ohioan's loyalty is a kind of composite conception, as of two in one—"*Imperium in imperio*"—which has slowly and insensibly formed itself from contemplation of the historical development of State and Union—the causative influences in whose ascendency nowhere appear so inveterately and inseparably interwoven as here—and to this unique devotion, in which dual sentiments reciprocally reenforce each other, we must look for a factor, not by any means the least, in the constitution of the Ohio man's political prowess, and in the commonwealth's pronounced prestige.

INDEX

Alger, General Russell A., 195, 295.
Allen, Ethan, 117.
Allen, William, 269, 298, 302.
Allyn, John, describes Connecticut in 1680, 24.
Ammen, Admiral Daniel, 284.
Anderson, Charles, 302.
Andrews, Sherlock J., 191.
Antislavery, idea of, actuates Connecticut men in war of rebellion, 47-49; David Wilmot, of Pennsylvania, and his Proviso, 122; Charles B. Storrs its pioneer in the Western Reserve, 174, 178; the general zeal for, in the West, 175, 178; services of Giddings and Wade for, in Western Reserve, 184, 185; John Brown's part, 189; Jacob Brinkerhoff's assistance to Wilmot, 190-191; at Oberlin, 199; cause of, as affected by the Ordinance of 1787, 219 *et seq.*; services of Ephraim Cutler for, in Ohio constitutional convention, 254; and of Edward Coles in Illinois, 255; Southern leaders of, in Ohio, 274-277; Clermont County as citadel of, 275-276. (See Slavery.)
"Appleseed, Johnny," 161-163.

Armstrong, Colonel John, 113-114.
Arnold, Benedict, 37.
Ashley, James A., 310.
Ashtabula County, Ohio, the "political Gibraltar" of the Western Reserve, 180.
Austin, Moses, projects colony in Texas, 29.
Austin, Stephen F., founds Texan city, 29.

Bacon, Delia S., 203.
Badger, Rev. Joseph, first preacher in Reserve, 158-159.
Baldwin, Michael, leads riot, 244, 245, 273.
Bancroft, H. H., 304.
Banning, General H. B., 281.
Bartley, Thomas W., 301.
Beard, David, 206.
Beard, James H., 206.
Beard, William H., 206.
Beatty, General John, 281.
Bebb, William, 301.
Bidlack, James, 91; killed by torture at Wyoming, 94.
Bierce, Ambrose, 205.
Bingham, John A., 266.
Birney, James G., 268, 276.
Bishop, R. M., 302.
Bolton, Sarah K., 205.

Ohio and Her Western Reserve

Brant, Joseph, Mohawk chief, mentioned, 80; with Indians at Tioga prior to Wyoming massacre, 84; mention of, 138; meets Western Reserve surveyors, 144.
Brant, Molly, 80.
Brinkerhoff, Henry, 191.
Brinkerhoff, Jacob, 190–191.
Brinkerhoffs, the, 272.
Brooks, General T. H., 281.
Brough, John, 189, 194, 284, 236, 302.
Brown, Ethan A., 300.
Brown, John, 189, 275.
Brush, Charles F., 207.
Buck, Aholiab, 91.
"Buckeye," origin of, 228.
Buckingham, General C. P., 281.
Buckingham, Governor William A., of Connecticut, 40.
Buell, General D. C., 281.
Burnet, Judge Jacob, 241; author of Ohio's first constitution, 255–256, 267, 298.
Burns, General W. W., 281.
Burrows, Julius Cæsar, 192, 296.
Bushnell, Asa S., 303.
Butler, Colonel John, mentioned, 82, 83; described, 85, 86, 88; in battle of Wyoming, 92, 93.
Butler, Colonel Zebulon, leader of Wyoming settlers, 69, 73; defeats Plunkett expedition, 77; becomes commander at Wyoming in hour of danger, 81; leads settlers in defense of Wyoming, 91, 92; arrested by Pennsylvanians, 112; for conciliation, 119.

Campbell, Alex., 297.
Campbell, James E., 302.

"Campus Martius," 228.
Canals, opening of Erie and Ohio, 154, 155.
Carlyle, Thomas, on Puritanism, 6–7.
Carter, Lorenzo, 148–149.
Cary sisters, 303.
Case, Leonard, 209.
Cass, Lewis, 271.
Catherwood, Mrs. Mary H., 304.
Chambers, Julius, 305.
Chapman, Jonathan, 161–163.
Chase, Salmon P., 271, 285, 291, 292, 293, 298, 301.
Chillicothe, settled by Virginians, 233, 234; becomes capital, 287; riotous demonstration in, against St. Clair, 244.
Chisholm, Henry, 208.
Cincinnati, first settlement of, 229.
Cist, Lewis J., quotations from, 51, 127.
Cleaveland, General Moses, mentioned, 140, 143–144, 147.
Clermont County, an antislavery citadel, 275–276.
Cleveland (city), surveyors at site of, 146–147; first residents of, 147 et seq; benefited by opening of canals, 154–153; Western Reserve University in, 197-198; marvelous growth and importance of, 208; the Boston of the West, 209.
Cockerill, John A., 305.
Coffin, Levi, 269.
Coles, Edward, 255.
Congregationalism, established religion in Connecticut, 32; in the Western Reserve, 173, 174.

Index

Conneaut, Reserve surveyors at, 144-146.
Connecticut, New. (See Western Reserve.)
Connecticut, Puritanism in, 3; first settlements of, 13, 14; first constitution of, 15-20; signal service of, to America, 20-21; influence of, on colonial expansion, 23 et seq.; first colonies of, 24, 27, 28; described by Allyn, 24-25; prolific of public men, 29-30; in Revolutionary War, 35 et seq.; in war of rebellion, 39 et seq.; charter of, 58; charter claim of, in Pennsylvania, 59 et seq.; first emigrants from, to Pennsylvania, 67; extends government over Wyoming, 74; divested of title to Wyoming by "Trenton decree," 108; forms plan of government for new State at Wyoming, 119; contribution of eminent men to Pennsylvania, 122; probably gains "Western Reserve" in Ohio as result of "Pennamite Wars," 124-125; triumph of, in Ohio, 129 et seq.; cedes claim to Western lands, 131-132; makes a reservation, 134-135; sets apart "Fire Lands" for "Sufferers," 138-139; authorizes sale of "Western Reserve" lands, 139; reproduced in Western Reserve, 158 et seq.; names of, in Western Reserve, 165, 166; reflex tide brings educators to, from Western Reserve, 200-201; contributions of, to Ohio, 265.
Constitution of Connecticut, first in America, 15-20, 53; first of Ohio, 255-257.
Cooke, Eleutheros, 191, 272.
Cooke, Jay, 206, 207, 272, 285, 286.
Corwin, Thomas, on Ohio's constitution, 256; nativity of, 268, 292, 293, 298, 301, 310.
Cowles, Alfred, 305.
Cowles, Edwin, 306.
Cox, General Jacob Dolson, 195, 205, 272, 282, 294, 302.
Cox, Kenyon, 206.
Cromwell, Oliver, 23, 44.
Cushutunk, 54, 57, 66.
Custer, General George A., 272, 281, 283.
Cutler, Ephraim, carries Ohio convention for prohibition of slavery, 254-255.
Cutler, Rev. Manasseh, as agent of Ohio Land Company, 223; his agency in forming and passing the Ordinance of 1787, 224; votes in Congress for a small State, contrary to the Ordinance, 249.

Dahlgren, Mrs. M. V., 272.
Day, William R., 292, 295.
Delano, Columbus, 294.
Delaware Company, 26, 58, 66.
Democracy, dawn of, in America, 15. (See Jeffersonian Democracy.)
Denham, Obed, 276.
Dennison, Colonel Nathan, 91, 92.
Dennison, William, 268, 284, 286, 293, 301.
Denver, James W. (note), 296.
Dewey, General Joel A., 195.

Ohio and Her Western Reserve

Dorrance, Lieutenant-Colonel George, 91; killed at Wyoming, 93.
Durkee, Colonel John, 91.
Durkee, Robert, 91.

Edison, Thomas A., 207.
Edwards, Pierpont, 139, 141.
Elkins, Stephen B., 291-292, 294.
Ellis, Edward S., 204.
Erie Canal, opening of, 154.
Erie Literary Society, 159-160.
Ewing, General Hugh B., 281.
Ewing, General Thomas H., 281.
Ewing, Thomas, 266, 292, 293.
Ewing, Thomas H., 293, 298.
Expansion, colonial, of Connecticut, 23 *et seq.*, 53, 60, 62; a persistent dream of, realized, 211.

Fairchild, James H, 200.
Fearing, Paul, 247, 297.
Federalists, from New England at Marietta, 235; downfall of, in West complicated with movement for Ohio statehood, 238 *et seq.*; pass a bill for erection of Ohio as a small State, 242; and a bill for removal of capital from Chillicothe to Cincinnati, 243; riot precipitated by these measures and St. Clair's unpopularity, 244; plans of, for State presented to Congress, 247; scheme of, defeated in Congress, 249; ludicrous objections of, to Ohio statehood, 251, 252; have only one official in first State government, 259.
Finney, Rev. Charles G., 200.

"Fire Lands," 138, 139, 166, 167;
Foraker, J. B., 300, 302.
Ford, Seabury, 194, 301.
Forsythe, General J. W., 281.
Fort Harmar, 227.
Fort Penn, 97, 100.
"Forty Fort," built in Wyoming by Connecticut settlers, 69; Wyoming men muster at, 90.
Foster, Charles, 291, 294, 302.
Franklin, Colonel John, 112, 120.
French in Ohio, 272.
Fullerton, A. J., 304.

Gallatin, Albert, service of, to Ohio in internal improvements, 259-260, 262.
Garfield, James A., 192, 195, 198, 272, 281, 286, 288, 289, 291, 299, 310.
Garrard, General K, 281.
Garrett, Major John, 91, 92, 93.
Geer, Rezin, 91.
Germans in Ohio, 272.
Gertrude of Wyoming, 103.
Giddings, Joshua R., mentioned, 174, 178, 180; birth and parentage of, 181; succeeds Whittlesey in Congress, 184; declares against slavery in Republican platform, 184; character of, 185-188; grave of, in Jefferson, 188; mentioned, 270, 275.
Governors, powers of Ohio's, limited, 256, 257; first of, 258; list of Ohio's, 300 *et seq.*
Granger, General Robert S., 281.
Granger, Gideon, 141.
Grant, General U. S., 273, 280, 291, 292, 293.
Greenville, treaty of, 138.

Index

Griffin, General Charles, 281.
Griswold, Harley, 191.
Griswold, Stanley, 297.

Hallam, Henry, on Puritanism, 6.
Halstead, Murat, 268.
Hamer, Thomas L., 266.
Hammond, Charles S., 268.
Hanna, M. A., 191, 300.
Harmon, Judson, 295.
Harrison, Benjamin, 290, 294.
Harrison, William Henry, 238; nativity of, 265; mentioned, 291, 297, 298.
Hartford, Conn., first settlement of, 14.
Harvey, Thomas W., 202–203.
Hatton, Frank, 294.
Hayes, Rutherford B., 271, 281, 289, 291, 294, 302.
Hay, John, 206.
Haydn, Rev. H. C., 197.
Hendricks, Thomas A., 291.
Hewitt, Dethic, 91.
Hickok, Laurens P., 198.
Hinsdale, Burke A., 198, 205.
Hiram College, 198.
Hitchcock, Peter, 191.
Hoadley, George, 270, 302.
Hooker, Rev. Thomas, settles in Hartford, Conn., 14; grave of, 14; inspires first written American Constitution, 16, 22, 46, 178.
Howells, W. D., 204, 304.
Hudson, David, 160.
Hume, David, on Puritanism, 5, 6.
Huntington, General Jedediah, 223.
Huntington, Samuel (Governor of Connecticut), 37, 39.

Huntington, Samuel (Governor of Ohio), 149–151; attacked by wolves, 156; second elected Governor of Ohio, 194; one of first judges of Supreme Court of Ohio, 259; mentioned, 270, 300.
Hutchins, John, 191.

Indians, sell lands to Connecticut settlers, 63, 66; massacre settlers at Wyoming (1762), 68; repudiate sale of lands, 69; concentrate at Tioga to move against Wyoming 81; descend on Wyoming, 89; in battle, 93; torture and kill captives, 95; release title to Ohio lands, 138; meet Connecticut emigrants, 144; the battles with St. Clair and Wayne, 231.
Irish, the, in Ohio, 273.

Jeffersonian Democracy, nucleus of Western, at Chillicothe, 234; rise of, complicated with statehood of Ohio, 238 *et seq.*; opposes Federalist measures, 243; antagonism of, to latter reaches riot, 244; takes active measures to control Ohio's formation, 245, 246; victory of, in Congress on Ohio statehood, 249, 250; controls first Ohio convention, 252; fills all State offices save one, 258, 259.
Jefferson, Thomas, urges settlement of Connecticut-Pennsylvania land claims, 111; and ordinance for the Northwest Territory, 224; interested in creation of Ohio as a State, 234, 243; sees

Ohio and Her Western Reserve

need of additional electoral votes, 246; attitude of, toward St. Clair, 248; removes St. Clair from office, 252-253.
Jefferson (town of), 183, 187-188.
Jenkins's Fort, 90.
Jennings, Rev. I., 202.
Jewett, Hugh J., 268.
Johnson, Sir William, 80.
Johnson, Tom L., 191.
Jones, Sir William, quoted, 213.

Keep, " Father " John, 200, 274.
Keifer, General J. W., 281.
Kelley, Alfred, 208, 270.
Kennan, George, 206.
Kentucky, contributions of, to Ohio, 268.
Kingsbury, Colonel James, 147-148, 149.
Kirker, Thomas, 300.
Kirtland, Jared P., 208.

Ladd, Rev. George T., 201, 205.
Lake Erie College, 200.
Lee, General John S., 281.
Lewis, Alfred Henry, 206.
Longworth, Nicholas, 267.
Looker, Othniel, 300.
Lowell, James Russell, quoted, 2, 170.
Lucas, Robert, 265, 301.
Lundy, Benjamin, 267, 275.
Lytle, General William H., 266, 281, 304.

McArthur, Duncan, 271, 300.
Macaulay, T. B., on Puritanism, 5.
McClellan, General George B., 282.
McCook, General A. McD., 281.
McCook, General Daniel, 281.

McCook, General Robert L., 281.
McCooks, " the fighting," 267, 273, 281.
McDowell, Irvin, 268, 273, 281.
MacGahan, J. A., 273.
McKarrican, William, 91.
McKinley, William, 192, 267, 291, 295, 303, 310.
McLean, General N. C., 281.
McLean, John, 267, 292, 293.
McMillan, William, 297.
McPherson, General J. B., 272, 273, 281.
Marietta, mentioned, 31; first settlers arrive at, 226, 227-228; Federal government organized at, 229-230.
Marshall, John, services of, to Western Reserve, 153.
Maryland, her " pioneer thought," 222; contributions of, to Ohio, 265, 268.
Mason, General J. S., 281.
Massachusetts, noble history of, 3; agency of, in giving law to the West, 235; contributions of men to Ohio, 270.
Massie, Nathaniel, 233.
Mather (clerical family), 141.
Mathews, Samuel H., inscription, iii.
Matthews, Stanley J., 292, 299.
Medill, William, 301.
Meigs, Return J., 269, 292, 297, 300.
Mentor, home of Garfield, 151.
Miller, Rear-Admiral J. N., 284.
Miller, W. H. H., 290, 295.
Mitchell, General John G., 281.
Mitchell, General O. M., 282.
Monroe, James, 191.

Index

Montour, Catharine, influential with Indians descending on Wyoming, 87, 88; in battle of Wyoming, 92; tomahawks sixteen captives, 95.
Morris, Thomas, 276, 277, 298.
Morrow, Jeremiah, 266, 297, 300.

Nash, George K., 303.
Natchez, Miss., a Connecticut settlement, 27.
Newberry, J. S., 208.
New England, Ohio Land Company of, 223; how composed, 225; virtually dictates passage of Ordinance of 1787, 226; contributions of, to Ohio, 269-271.
New Jersey, contributions of, to Ohio, 265, 267.
New York, contributions of, to Ohio, 265, 271.
Noble, John W., 290, 295.
Northaway, Stephen A., 191.
North Carolina, contributions of, to Ohio, 268.
Northwest Territory, 229; first officials of, 230; population of, in 1790, 231; government of, advanced to second phase, 237; plans for division of, 241-243.
Noyes, Edward F., 302.

Oberlin, 174, 175, 199-200.
Ochs, Adolph S., 305.
Ogden, Amos, 69, 70, 73.
Ohio, a complicated study, 215; the product of a happy conjunction of causes, 217, 218; its settlement projected by patriots under the counsel of Washington, 218; the "Ordinance of Freedom" the first favoring cause of the State's prosperity, 219; not a sporadic growth, 219; the ordinance an agency for "selection," of people, 220-221; history of the ordinance, 222 et seq.; Rev. Manasseh Cutler and the Ordinance of 1787, 223-224; Washington upon the settlement of, at Marietta, 225; first settlement of, 226, et seq.; significance of "Buckeye," 228; settlement of Cincinnati, 229; government of Territory organized at Marietta, 229-230; St. Clair's and Wayne's campaigns against the Indians, 231; great accessions to population of, in 1796, 232-233; Virginia Military District, 232; Chillicothe settled, 233; Virginians credited with giving Ohio statehood, 234, 235; statehood not achieved at a stroke, 236; statehood linked with rise of Jeffersonian Democracy, 237; statehood hastened by animosity to St. Clair, 238-240; and by advance of Territorial government to second form, 241; smallness of the State proposed by Federalists, 242, 243; riotous demonstrations caused by statehood agitation, 244; Worthington goes to Washington in interests of State creation, 245; struggle for statehood wholly one of partizan politics, 246; the battle in Washington, 247; and in the Territory, 248; Federalist plan for State rejected by Congress,

Ohio and Her Western Reserve

249; "Enabling Act" passes Congress for admission of State, 249; tables completely turned against Federalists, 250; grounds of Federalists' protest, 251-252; St. Clair dismissed from office by President Jefferson, 253; free-soil provision of Ordinance of 1787 attacked in constitutional convention, 253; but signally and successfully defended by Ephraim Cutler, 254-255; first constitution's authorship, 255-256; limitation of executive's power, 256-257; admission of State unique, 257; various dates of State's origin, 258; Albert Gallatin's service to Ohio, 259-260, 262; ascendency of State analyzed, 261 *et seq.*; causes of growth, 261-262; settlement from all of the States, 263; contributions from leading ones, 265 *et seq.*; contributions from New England. 269-271; nationalities represented in population, 272-273; War of 1812 as cause of State's growth, 273-274; earnestness of political convictions, 274; prominence of Southern antislavery men, 274-277; progress of population, 278; the State in war of the rebellion, 279 *et seq.*; generals of, 280 *et seq.*; civilians prominent in war period, 284 *et seq.*; prominence of Ohioans in post-bellum civil affairs, 287 *et seq.*; Ohioans at inauguration of Garfield, 288-289; great number of Ohio-born Congressmen in service, 290; disguised Ohioans in Harrison's Cabinet, 290; remarkable roster of Ohioans in national offices, 291 *et seq.*; same arranged by administrations, 292 *et seq.*; Senators, 296; Governors, 300; literature and authors, 303; journalists, 305; artists, 306; scientists, 306; *résumé* of causes of Ohio's prestige, 307 *et seq.*; vote of State, how cast, 308; as an "October State," 309; long terms of Senators and Representatives, 310-311; population, 312-314; Ohio's contributions to the building of other States, 313; State motto, 315; conclusion, 316.

Opdyke, General Emerson, 195, 281.
Opper, Frederick, 206.
Ordinance of 1787, the, as the first cause of Ohio's favorable foundation, 219; establishes "freedom forever" northwest of the Ohio, 219; becomes more valuable to Ohio as an agency for selecting its population, 220; history of its formation and enactment, 222 *et seq.*; why it passed, 223; Manasseh Cutler's authorship of, 224; virtually dictated by land purchasers, 226; integrity of, attacked in Ohio's first convention, 253; but successfully defended by Ephraim Cutler, 254-255; principles of, advanced by Southern men in Ohio, 274-277.

Paine, Eleazar A., 195.
Paine family, 151.

Index

Paine, General Edward, 149.
Paine, Halbert E., 195.
Painesville, founded, 151.
Parsons, General Samuel Holden, 148, 230.
Payne, Henry B., 191, 299.
"Pennamite Wars," allusion to, 56; keynote of, 64; real beginning of, 69; Ogden arrests "Yankee" settlers, 70; Captain Lazarus Stewart assists colonists, 71; first blood flows, 72; Wyoming colony wiped out, 73; Connecticut supports her colonists and extends government over them, 74; become complicated with Revolution, 75; Plunkett's expedition, 75-77; connection of, with Revolution, 79; reopening of, under new conditions, 111; Patterson's exploits in, 112-114; civil war and new State threatened, 115-116; Timothy Pickering's diplomacy, 118; progress of "new State" idea, 119-120; Compromise Act, 120-121; results of war to Pennsylvania, 122, 123; a final result of, is gaining of "Western Reserve" by Connecticut, 124-125.
Pendleton, George H., 299.
Pennsylvania, charter of, explained, 61; Connecticut settlers in, 54, 57; prepares to resist Connecticut invasion, 66; first "Yankee" settlers in, 67; attitude of, to Wyoming, 106; title to Wyoming lands vested in, 108; takes measures against Wyoming settlers, 111-114; reluctantly concedes individual title to Connecticut men at Wyoming, 118, 119; results to, of "Pennamite War," 122; votes for grant to Connecticut from Western lands, 135; contributions of, to Ohio, 265, 266.
Perkins, Joseph, 208.
Perry, Oliver Hazard, victory of, 154.
Phelps, Oliver, 141.
Piatt, General A. S., 281.
Piatts, the, 267.
Pickering, Timothy, as diplomat in Wyoming troubles, 117-118; arrested by Connecticut men, 120, 243.
Politics: new Western Democracy forms nucleus at Chillicothe, 234; Federalists from New England in Ohio, 235; Ohio comes naturally by predilection for, 236; war of Federalists and Jeffersonian Republicans over statehood for Ohio, 238 *et seq.*; partizan measures of Ohio Federalists, 242, 243; Jeffersonians plan Ohio as a partizan State, 246; Thomas Worthington visits national capital, 247; battle for statehood given additional heat by opposition to St. Clair, 248 *et seq.*; Federalist plans for State defeated, 249; pro and con of statehood agitation, 251-252; Jeffersonians fill all State offices but one, 258-259; earnestness in, a cause of development of State power, 274; Southern antislavery leaders prominent in Ohio, 274-277; election

Ohio and Her Western Reserve

of Brough, over Vallandigham, 284; prominence of Ohio in national civil affairs, 287 *et seq.*; roster of officials in Federal and State service for one hundred years, 291 *et seq.*; causes of political prestige of State, 307; vote of State since 1824, 308; Ohio an "October State," 309; long terms of office an element of strength, 308, 309, 310. (See Jeffersonian Democracy, Federalists, etc.)

Potts, General B. F., 281.
Powers, Hiram, 306.
Pugh, Achilles, 266, 275.
Pugh, George E., 299.
Puritanism, seamy side of, 4–5; British historians on, 5–7; attitude of, toward literature, 8–9; progressive character of, in America, 11, 20–21; relaxes in West, 31–32; and "coolness of judgment," 35; outcome of, in Connecticut, 45; in the Western Reserve, 169, 171; progressive nature of, in the West, 172 *et seq.*; mingled with patriotism forms code of moral aggression in Western Reserve, 177; idea of, put in force by Giddings and Wade, 178 *et seq.*
Putnam, General Israel, 37, 43.
Putnam, General Rufus, 223, 226.

"Queen Esther." (See Montour, Catharine.)

Rankin, John, 276.
Ranney, Rufus P., 194.
Ransom, Samuel, 91.

Rebellion, War of, Connecticut in 39 *et seq.*; Ohio in, 279 *et seq.*
Reid, Whitelaw, 273, 305.
Reilly, General J. W., 195, 282.
Republicans. (See Jeffersonian Democracy, Politics, etc.)
Revolutionary War, Connecticut in, 35 *et seq.*; Wyoming's rank in, 102; Ohio pioneers officers in, 225, 226.
Rhodes, James Ford, 205.
Rice, Harvey, 202.
Riddle, Albert Gallatin, 191, 203.
Robinson, General J. S., 282.
Roosevelt, Theodore, on Ohio's first constitution, 256.
Rosecrans, General W. S., 267, 273, 281.
Root, Joseph M., 191.
Ruggles, James M. (note), 296.
Runkle, General B. P., 282.
Rusk, Jeremiah M., 290, 295.
Russell, A. P., 304.

St. Clair, General Arthur, as Governor of the Northwest Territory, 230; defeat of, by Indians, 231; unpopularity of, 238; animosity toward him hastens formation of State, 238 *et seq.*; death of, 241; riotous demonstration against, 244; denounced by Jeffersonians as an aristocrat and tyrant, 248; makes injudicious speech to Legislature, 252; removed from office by President Jefferson, 253; shadow of, falls on Ohio's constitution, 257.
Sargent, Winthrop, 230.
Schenck, General Robert C., 281.

Index

Scotch-Irish, the, in Ohio, 273.
Senators of United States from Ohio, 296.
" Seven Ranges," 233.
" Shades of Death," flight of Wyoming settlers through, 98.
Shannon, Wilson, 273, 300.
Shaw, Albert, 305.
Sheridan, General P. H., 273, 280, 283, 289.
Sherman, John, 270, 271, 286, 289, 291, 292, 294, 295; long term of, 299 (note), 311.
Sherman, General William T., 289, 292, 294.
Sill, General Joshua, 282.
Six Nations, lands of, purchased, 63; prepare to descend on Wyoming, 78, 79, 80, 81, 89, 90, 93.
Slavery, prohibited in Northwest Territory by Ordinance of 1787, 219-221; limited plan of, proposed for Ohio, 253; but defeated in convention by Ephraim Cutler, 254, 255; vote on, in Ohio convention, 254. (See Antislavery.)
Sloan, John, 191.
Sloane, William M., 304.
Slough, General John P., 282.
Smith, General W. S., 282.
Smith, John, 297.
Spalding, Rufus P., 191.
Sparks, Edwin E., 305.
Spencer, Platt R., 207.
Sproat, Colonel Ebenezer, 228.
Stanberry, Henry, 271, 293.
Stanley, General David S., 281.
Stanton, Edwin M., 268, 286, 291, 292, 293.

Statistics: of Western Reserve's growth, 153, 210; of Cleveland's growth, 208; of Ohio's progress in population, 278, 312; of population contributed to other States, 313-314 (note); and of those received from other States and nations, 314 (note).
Steedman, General Jacob D., 273, 282.
Stewart, Lazarus, 71, 91.
Stone, Amasa, 209.
Storrs, Charles B., 47, 174, 178, 274.
" Sufferers' Lands." (See " Fire Lands.")
Susquehanna Company, the, 63, 65.
Swan, Joseph R., 271.
Swayne, General John Wager, 281.
Swayne, Noah H., 265, 292.
Symmes, John Cleves, 229, 230, 267.

Taft, Alphonso, 294.
Tappan, Benjamin, 298.
Taylor, Ezra B., 191.
Teedyuscung, Delaware chief, burned to death, 67-68.
Thomas, Edith, 204.
Thurman, Allen G., 266, 267, 291, 299.
Thwing, Rev. Charles F., 197.
Tiffin, Edward, first Governor of Ohio, 258, 272, 297, 300.
Tioga, Indians concentrate at, 81-83.
Tod, David, 194, 270, 284, 286, 301.
Tories, expelled from Wyoming, 79; with British and Indians in

Ohio and Her Western Reserve

attack on Wyoming, 81–82; in England, affected by Wyoming massacre, 102.
Tourgee, Albion W., 205.
" Trenton Decree," 108 *et seq.*
Trimble, Allen, 265, 300.
Trimble, William, 298.
Trumbull County organized, 152.
Trumbull, Jonathan, 36, 37, 132.

" Underground Railroad," 175, 199.
Upson, William H., 191.

Vallandigham, Clement L., 194, 284.
Vance, Joseph, 266, 301.
Van De Veer, General F., 282.
Varnum, James M., 230.
Venable, W. H., 304.
Vermont, immigrants from, to Ohio, 271.
Vinton, Samuel F., 271.
Virginia, Congressmen of, opposed to granting Connecticut's Western Reserve, but vote for, 136; reserves military lands in Ohio, 232; her people dominate early Ohio, 233 *et seq.*; settlers from, give Ohio its statehood, 234 *et seq.*; contributions from, to Ohio, 265–266; antislavery leaders from, in Ohio, 275–276.

Wade, Benjamin F., mentioned, 164, 178, 180; birth and parentage of, 182–183; in United States Senate, 185; character of, 185–188; grave of, in Jefferson, 188; mentioned, 265, 270, 285, 291, 299, 311.

Wade, Edward, 183, 191.
Wade, General M. S., 282.
Wade, J. H., 209.
Waite, Morrison R., 270, 289, 292.
Ward, J. Q. A., 306.
Ware, Eugene F., quoted, 213.
Warner, General W., 282.
War of 1812, effects of, on Ohio, 273.
Warren, first seat of justice in Western Reserve, 152.
" Warrior's Path," 99.
Washington, George, moves for avenging of Wyoming, 105; opposed to grant of Western Reserve, 136; counsels settlement of Ohio, 218; upon the West, 225; upon Arthur St. Clair, 240.
Wayne, General Anthony, chastises Indians and makes treaty of Greenville, 138.
Weitzel, General Godfrey, 281.
Western Reserve College (and University), mentioned, 159, 160, 174, 178; organized at Hudson, 196; removed to Cleveland, 197, 198.
Western Reserve, mentioned, 28, 110; gained by Connecticut through conditions at Wyoming, 124–125; triumph of Connecticut in, 129 *et seq.*; Connecticut cedes claim to Western lands, 131–132; a " reserve " stipulated, 132; reasons for same, 133; based on Wyoming, 134; Washington opposed to grant of, 136; Virginia Congressmen originally oppose, but finally vote for, 136; reasons therefor, 137; Indian title to,

Index

secured, 138; the "Fire Lands" set apart, 138-139; sale of lands in, 139 et seq.; personnel of purchasers, 140; General Moses Cleaveland, 143-144; the surveyors, 144; Fourth of July, 1796, at Coṅneaut, "the Plymouth of the West," 144-146; surveyors at site of Cleveland, 146-147; first residents, 147 et seq.; local government established, 152; John Marshall's great service to, 153; Perry's victory, 154; benefited by opening of Erie Canal, 154; and by Ohio Canal, 155; safety and peacefulness of life in, 155-157; as a conservation of Connecticut, 158 et seq.; first preacher in, 158; first school in, 159, 160; its local character "Johnny Appleseed," 161-163; irreligion and whisky drinking in, 163-164; pioneer teachers of, paid in whisky, 164; Connecticut names in, 165-166; map of, 167; amount and division of lands in, 166-168; counties of, 168; distinctness of, as a Connecticut colony, 169; force of heredity in, 170; Puritanism modified in, 171-173; progression and radicalism of, 172-177; Mormonism given short shrift in, 176; Puritanism influences politics in, 177; rise of antislavery, 177 et seq.; called "a State separate from Ohio," 179; Giddings and Wade, 180 et seq.; John Brown, 189; contributions of, to national service, 190 et seq.; James A. Garfield, 192; William McKinley, 192; contributions to civil roster of State, 193-195; governors from, 194; civil-war generals from, 195; education, 196; "Yale of the West" at Hudson, 196; University of, in Cleveland, 197, 198; Hiram and Wooster Colleges, 198; Oberlin, 199-200; Lake Erie College, 200; reflex tide among educators, 200-201; the common schools, 201-203; literature and authors, 203 et seq.; growth of Cleveland, 208; commercial importance of Cleveland, 208, 209; comparison of, with several States, 210; conclusion, 211: mentioned, 232, 233, 265, 269.

Whittlesey, Asaph, 191.
Whittlesey, Charles, 208.
Whittlesey, Elisha, 184, 191.
Wilkesbarre, first settlement of, 67; the town named, 74.
Wilmot, David, author of "Proviso," 122, 191, 192.
Windom, William, 290, 294.
Winsor, Justin, quoted, 27.
Wintermoot's Fort, 90.
Wolcott, Governor, on Connecticut colonists in Pennsylvania, 64; writes constitution for new "Yankee" State in Pennsylvania, 119.
Wolcutt, General C. C., 282.
Wood Reuben, 194, 271, 301.
Woods, General C. R., 282.
Woods, General W. B., 282, 292.
Woolsey, Sarah C., 205.
Woolson, Constance F., 205.
Worthington, Thomas, chief pro-

moter of Ohio's statehood, 244–245; goes to Washington in its interest, 245; his labor there, 247; mentioned, 265, 297, 300.

Wright, G. Frederick, 206, 208.

Wyoming, as "Windsor of the West," 24, 27, 57; first settled, 67; first massacre at, 68; great growth of, 75; Indian hostility to, 78; signs of danger at, increase, 80; Indians advance upon, 89, 90; battle of, 192 *et seq.*; massacre begins, 94; captive inhabitants tortured and killed, 95; total losses in battle and massacre of, 96; flight from, 96–98; far-reaching effects of battle, 101 *et seq.*; ranked with Lexington and Concord in significance, 102; attention of world drawn to, 103, 104; settlers return to, 105; Connecticut and Pennsylvania claims to lands of, left to adjudication, 106; commissioners appointed, 107; lands of, vested in Pennsylvania, 108; Wyoming men acquiesce, 110; as nucleus of proposed new State, 116; lands of, finally confirmed to "Yankee" settlers, 122; contest for results in Connecticut gaining the "Western Reserve," 124–125, 134–136.

"Yale of the West." (See Western Reserve College.)

Young, John, founds Youngstown, 151–152.

Young, Thomas L., 302.

Youngstown founded, 151.

Zanes, the, 267.

THE END

www.ingramcontent.com/pod-product-compliance
Lightning Source LLC
Chambersburg PA
CBHW051626230426
43669CB00013B/2200